The Pursuit of Purpose

by Ron Ball

© Copyright 2021 Ron Ball

All rights reserved.

No part of this publication may be reproduced, in whole or in part, stored in a retrieval system, or transmitted in any form or by any means - electronic, mechanical, digital, photocopy, recording or any other - without prior written permission of the publisher.

ISBN: 978-1-64142-317-5

Introduction

7

Chapter 1

Finding Your Fit

9

Chapter 2

The Purpose of Success

21

Chapter 3

Signals

41

Chapter 4

What's in Your Box?

69

Chapter 5

The Goal Ladder

73

Chapter 6

The Goal Explosion

107

Chapter 7

The Desires of Your Heart

121

Chapter 8

How to Avoid Purpose Blockage

145

Chapter 9

How to Lock onto Your Purpose

165

Introduction

I have great news for you!

You are holding a book that answers the questions you really care about. Why are you here? What does your life mean? What is your true purpose?

This book offers vital answers. It is a roadway into romance, adventure, and happiness. It is a pathway into your exciting purpose. Much has been written about goal setting and dream-building. Books are available that can teach you the techniques of time management and the development of success habits. All of this is valuable and important, but have you ever wondered what this information is for? Do you need to understand how to make your life mean more than just the accomplishment of measurable objectives? Is your life more than the possessions you own? Is it really all about you?

The following chapters offer my personal perspective on how I came to discover my own purpose. Although my experiences may differ from yours, they contain principles that I believe can guide you to yours. I deeply believe that a personal and active God made you for a reason. I believe that He allowed you to be born when and where you entered the world because you are needed for something that matters. You are that important.

This is a "guidebook" into a goal-setting system that can not only help you accomplish your dreams but can also use your goals to lead you the grandest goal of all, the fulfillment of your true purpose.

It is not wrong to work for personal rewards and income. It is not wrong to enjoy the "fruits" of your labor. But when you add your purpose to those "lesser" goals, your life will explode with power and blessing. Your blessings will overflow into the lives of others. You will be happy and fulfilled because you will be doing what you were born to do.

Are you ready to start? Your purpose awaits.

CHAPTER 1
Finding Your Fit

The Wrong Sport

basketball my freshman year and decided to switch to football. My decision was not based on a desire to play a particular sport. It was based on a desire to meet and impress girls. I had noticed that the girls in our school were more attracted to the football players than basketball players.

When I arrived for the first practice session, I realized that my size would be a problem. I was five feet six inches tall and weighed 125 pounds. The team members I met were all taller, bigger, stronger, and faster than me. At the end of the practice I was battered, bruised and sore. I hurt so much I could barely walk home. When I (slowly) entered my home, my mother was shocked and asked if I had been in an accident.

At the practice, the following day, I worked hard to learn the routines and routes but still was repeatedly thrown to the ground with bruises on top of my bruises. My small size made it impossible to compete physically with the other players.

I pushed and fought but could not overcome my physical limitations. By the end of the week, I knew that I did not "fit at football" I also realized that no girl was worth the punishment I had to endure.

I was still determined not to quit when my parents informed me that the head coach had called them and asked to meet with me. At the meeting the coach confirmed what I already suspected that I was not physically suited for football. After thanking me for my commitment and effort, he said that it would benefit everyone if I dropped the sport. He made it clear that I did not "fit".

I eventually found another sport for which I was more physically suited. I played soccer in college and, to my surprise, found that most girls were certainly attracted to soccer players. Everything ended well.

Before you find your **purpose,** you need to find your **fit.** You need to locate the best place where you can excel and succeed. You need to do something that flows from your natural gifts and abilities. You need to "find your fit".

The Piece of the Puzzle

Our young grandson recently discovered shapes and colors. He quickly realized that a round peg would not fit in a square hole. To complete a puzzle, each piece should rest in its correct place.

The same is true for you. When you try to force yourself to do a job that is not a natural fit, you experience frustration and disappointment. Even when you try to do the job well, you will always be less than the person who "fits" the job. Jim Collins, in his influential book, From *Good to Great*, says that most businesses fail to reach "greatness" because too many people are in positions that don't fit their personalities and skills. They may work hard enough to "be good", but they will never "be great."

When you push yourself into areas that don't fit who you are, you create unnecessary pressure and drain your energy. You become a candidate for early burn-out. Isn't it better to find the place where you can love what you do?

You can miss your purpose because your focus is fractured by your failure to fit. When you are forced to give your attention to the wrong job, you often don't have the energy left to do the right job.

The Song Leader Who Couldn't Sing

When I was in college, I was asked to lead the music at a church conference. When the speaker contacted me, I told him that I had no musical ability and "could not carry a tune". He said that he urgently needed someone to help him and believed that because I was outgoing and "had a lot of energy", I "could do it". I reluctantly agreed.
On the night of the conference, I introduced the first song to the audience but, because I had no training or ability, I did what was natural for me. I talked about the history and meaning of the song. I delayed if I could the moment when I would have to sing.
Finally, I opened my mouth and the disaster I expected quickly happened. I continued to explain the next three songs and continued to destroy the music. I spent over an hour explaining the songs (which was my strength) and singing (painfully). By the time I finished, the program was over, and the speaker had no time left to speak.
After we left the building, the speaker confronted me. He was blazing with anger. He told me I had ruined the program, embarrassed him and that my singing was atrocious (I already knew that). I apologized and, politely, reminded him that I had told him I could not lead music and that it was a mistake to put me in charge of that part of the program. It took months for our relationship to recover.
This is a classic "fish out of water" story. I was the wrong person doing the wrong job. I should never have agreed to his proposal.
There may be some jobs that you can learn well enough to be acceptable, but you will never be as good as someone who has a natural affinity for that position. It will take more effort and more time for you to do what another person could do quickly and efficiently.

The Frustrating Christmas Tree

Every year, my wife Amy, puts up an artificial Christmas tree in early November (she loves Christmas). Just after Thanksgiving, she follows the first tree with a fresh, live tree (while keeping the first tree).
One year my son Jonathan and I brought the live tree home and prepared to place it in the house. We laid the tree on our front porch so that the bottom of the trunk was suspended over the edge of the porch. Jonathan, by tradition, always cuts off the bottom of the tree, so I handed him the same saw we had used the previous year.
I firmly held down the tree while Jonathan started to slice through the trunk. Jonathan pushed with all his strength, but nothing happened. He used the same technique he had used before, but the saw would not move. Finally, with intense effort, he managed to move the saw enough to start the cut, but the saw would not penetrate any further.
I examined the saw and observed that the teeth were dull, and some parts were bent and useless. I realized that we needed a new saw. After I returned with the new implement, Jonathan easily carved through the tree. We planted it in its holder and decided that we would recheck the saw every year so that we always had the right tool for the job.
The problem was not Jonathan. The problem was the tool. Remember that you are the human tool that is applied to whatever job you do. When you are not the right tool, the job is much harder and demands more from you. You may even not be able to complete the job.

The Greek Temperaments

The early Greek physician Hippocrates taught that human beings were divided into four temperaments or "humors", which were understood as bodily fluids that carried certain characteristics.
According to Hippocrates, certain people were filled with **choleric** fluid

which made them forceful, confident, and aggressive. The choleric individual was seen as outgoing, commanding and goal centered. Others were dominated by **sanguine** fluid which cause them to be happy, flexible, social, fun-loving, and good communicators. The ones filled with **melancholic** fluid were usually thoughtful, introspective, sensitive, and artistic.

The final fluid, the **phlegmatic,** made people steady, cooperative, dependable, organized, and methodical. These temperaments or "humors", based on what Hippocrates believed were based on the predominance certain fluids that circulated the human body controlled the study of human personality for thousands of years.

In 1928, William Marston published, *Emotions of Normal People*, in which he introduced his definitions of the temperaments. He called his approach, "the DISC system". His system is divided into four types. The **Dominant** personality is confident, and goal centered. The **Influence** personality is open and relational. The **Steady** personality is dependable, cooperative, and sincere. The **Conscientious** personality is competent, accurate and organized.

When you compare Hippocrates and Marston, you can see the obvious similarities. Marston's system is still used effectively in business and personal development. Marston, a Harvard psychologist also, with the help of his wife, invented the lie detector and created the comic book character, Wonder Woman.

Donald Clifton, recognized by the American Psychological Association as "the father of strengths-based psychology and the grandfather of positive psychology", addressed the temperaments in different way. He focused on finding a person's positive strengths and building success in life on those strengths. As the Chairman of the Gallup Company, he popularized the idea of "strength-finders" (he called it "Clifton-strengths"). Clifton believed that most psychologists concentrated too much on people's problems and weaknesses. He decided to develop a tool that would help people discover and use their strengths. He identified 34 strengths and used a questionnaire to reveal those strengths. His research has been hugely influential in the personal development industry.

Carl Jung, along with Sigmund Freud, the most influential psychologist of the past 100 years, had an even simpler approach to the understanding of human behavior. He believed that everyone is divided into two types. You are either an **extrovert** or an **introvert.** Jung taught that everything about you starts with your type.

All of this is to help you understand yourself and "find your fit". There are other personality systems in addition to those I have described here. I chose these because they are simple, uncomplicated, and easy to follow. I also think they provide enough core knowledge to enable you to arrive at a basic understanding of your own personality.

With this as a background, I want to give you a list of the twelve most common leadership/personality types I have found. They are based on my own research and experience with thousands of the individuals with whom I have worked and interacted.

This is not the ultimate list. You may identify other types that you think should be included, but I believe that these twelve examples are enough for most of you to locate your specific type.

1. The Reacher

This is the high achiever who wakes up every morning with an inner fire. If you are a "Reacher", then every day starts at zero. You refuse to dwell on the past. You have a continual sense of "positive discontent" that keeps you from being easily satisfied. You need to accomplish something every day. You wrestle with the feeling that "nothing is ever enough". You may be insensitive to other people if they do not share your goals and you are happy to take leadership in any situation. You bring positive, "can-do" energy to every task. You simply believe that anything is possible. You are never satisfied until you see real results and what you set out to do is accomplished.

2. The Researcher

You are naturally analytical and will do nothing without proof. You always look for cause and effect. You want to know "why" something is the way it is. You can be content without an agenda if you are pursuing knowledge. You are happy if you are collecting data. You see structures and patterns that help you explain people and events. You enjoy breaking things down into their parts so you can see how they work. You can become so involved in your research that you lose track of the goal and cause people to be frustrated when you are slow to act (because you are so caught up in the accumulation of information.) You tend to love information for its own sake. Your biggest weakness is a tendency to become "trapped" inside your "information box" which can prevent you from seeing different possibilities. Your imagination can be overwhelmed by the amount of data you have uncovered.

3. The Manager

You see yourself as an "orchestra conductor" who is responsible for giving people direction. You are frustrated by disorganization. You are always looking for "the best way" to do something. You are quick to change plans if you think of a better one. You like to connect people to the jobs you think they are best suited for. You naturally see "the bigger picture" and easily focus on how all the pieces of a project (or a person) fit together. You don't always follow the accepted rules because your purpose is to find the best way to accomplish the goal.

4. The General

You automatically take charge of every situation. You move forward with no doubt or debate. You are certain of your opinions and believe completely in your judgment. You have no fear of confrontation and have no difficulty challenging and correcting people, although you must guard against being too harsh or critical. You take risks and push the people around you to do the same. You act without hesitation and deal with problems and emergencies immediately and decisively. You can make devastating mistakes because of your self-assurance and refusal to consider other viewpoints. Of all the types you most need the balance of humility. You need to listen to other people to protect your decision-making.

5. The Teacher

You enjoy understanding and explaining things. You are gifted in speaking and writing and communicate with clarity. You are energized by new ideas and love bringing those ideas to life in the lives of other people. You are a natural storyteller. You find communication so enjoyable that you can become lazy and inactive. Words and ideas can replace people and action. You need a motivating goal that inspires you to use your communication gifts for a higher purpose, otherwise you can lose yourself in communication as an end. You need to cause something to happen with your words or you become merely an entertainer.

6. The Rival

You see everything as a competition. You make like someone but still consider them a rival when you work together on a project. You have a constant need to prove yourself. Because you are a high performer, you raise the performance level of everyone else. You make your team better because you are always pushing to win. You promote excellence and demand competence. You help people understand where they are in their pursuit of a goal because you always measure performance. You always know what "has to be done" to succeed. You are "black and white". You either win or lose. There is no middle. You can be socially undeveloped because of your total goal-focus. This can cause you to cheat and abuse people to win. You can seriously damage relationships because of your compulsion to win. You need to balance love and leadership. Your competitive drive can help win the day, but you want to make sure your friends are still with you when you get there.

7. The Bridge-Builder

You love helping people. You are a connector and enjoy matching people so they can have good relationships. Your primary purpose is to influence people to work well together. You instinctively know how to create teams and believe everyone should support everyone else. You have goals but believe they are best reached together. The results are not worth it unless everyone shares in the reward. You are considerate, thoughtful, and caring. You dislike isolation and do not enjoy working alone. You are a healer and seek ways to turn confrontation into cooperation. Your biggest weakness is the temptation to sacrifice your beliefs and convictions so everyone can "get along." You need a clear moral radar that can guide you, so you don't compromise what matters.

8. The Diplomat

You always look for areas of agreement. You can submerge your ego for the greater good of the team. You avoid debate but encourage constructive discussion. You dislike confrontation and seek compromise. You never want to "rock the boat." You are sensitive to the "feeling" of harmony. You may avoid real issues to make it easier for everyone cooperate. Because of these problems may not be solved, only postponed. You are polite and always show good manners. You are skilled at hiding what you really think and can use words that camouflage what is really happening. Because of this you need to work on honesty and accuracy. You do not want to sacrifice what is right for the sake of harmony. You are usually calm and project a sense of peace and stability that helps decrease tension and help people relax. You have an ability to quickly see a person's strengths and weaknesses. You know how to make everyone think they have gained something.

9. The Friend

You make friends with everyone. You are comfortable with intimate conversation. You open your heart easily and share your feelings in an honest and positive way. You listen carefully and effectively. You love to give gifts and remember the special occasions in the lives of others. You always want a deeper relationship and are willing to work to make that happen. You truly care and express support and encouragement. You hate "fake relationships". You want only "real relationships." You quickly and easily forgive other people. You apologize when needed. You maintain contact when apart. You initiate and sustain connection. You are dependable and help when asked. You pray for people. You want to help people solve their problems. You care so much that if someone betrays your trust you may end the relationship because of your disappointment. You will forgive but find it difficult to continue the friendship. In your desire to support people, you may find it difficult to tell the truth when they need to hear it. Because of this lack of "tough love", you may make it harder for someone to overcome their challenges.

10. The Thinker

You love mental games and intellectual challenge. You enjoy the process of thinking and arrive at observations and conclusions that other people miss. You are careful and your decisions are based on facts. You eliminate emotion and see things logically and clearly. You see sequences, which means that you understand how and why one thing leads logically to the next thing. You love the process of thinking to such an extent that you can become so involved in your mental world that you forget and neglect people. Your logic can become cold and unfeeling. You need to remind yourself to consider peoples' emotional responses and needs. You tend to be introspective, and you disconnect from the outside world can prevent you from having a healthy balance. You have much to offer because of your mental skills but need to add an awareness of people to create your balance.

11. The Builder

To you, excellence is everything. You see every situation as an opportunity to elevate something and maximize its potential. You are unsatisfied with the current conditions around you and want to create improvement in everything. You are always in motion, adjusting and expanding everything to make it all better. You work fast and hate wasting time. You enjoy changing your environment, whether altering your clothing or moving your furniture to new positions. You love change because you believe everything can always be better. You are excited when you find something being underused or even abandoned because it gives you the chance to "save it". You especially enjoy re-purposing items and creating uses no one else saw. You are a refiner. You polish everything. You want to leave everything better than you found it including relationships. You hate to throw anything away because you think it will have an eventual use. You can be impatient with people who do not share your passion. You may become a hoarder and become nervous when not allowed to improve everything. You may even have trouble sleeping because your mind is always considering new projects.

12. The Seller

You live every day with high energy. You seek common ground with everyone you meet because it makes it easier to promote your ideas. You like people and "never meet a stranger". You are drawn to people who disagree with you because you want to "win them over." You don't argue, you persuade. You communicate with humor and passion. You are "the life of the party" and people enjoy your company. You talk easily and can smoothly adapt your conversational style to different people. You love meeting new people. You are never afraid or intimidated by anyone. Everyone you meet is a potential friend. You are verbal and expressive. You can "sell" whatever you are interested into anyone at any time. You can also be shallow because after you meet someone you easily lose interest in them and switch to the next new person. You need novelty and are easily bored. Because of this you may be erratic and undependable. When someone confronts you with these weaknesses you sincerely apologize and try to change but the discipline to do so is difficult (although not impossible).

You can see from this sample list that people come in all shapes, sizes, and types. The important thing for you to do is to use this information to focus on your strengths and find where you best fit. Finding your fit is the beginning of finding your purpose.

CHAPTER 2

The Purpose of Success

I was backstage at a coliseum in Charlotte, North Carolina. I was scheduled to speak later in the evening to over fifteen thousand people and had come to the event early to meet and hear a man who was a legend in his industry. I had heard audios of this man and been impressed with his ability to relate to everyone listening. I had read two of his books, both national bestsellers. Now I was going to meet this remarkable individual.

I waited in a private room, ready for his arrival. Soon the door opened, and the man walked into the room. Before I could introduce myself, the man smiled, introduced himself first and extended his hand. He radiated warmth and open friendliness. Although this man was far better known than me and exercised influence beyond my smaller orbit, he welcomed me as an equal and instantly put me at ease. For the next half-hour, he asked me questions about myself and offered to keep in contact. He and I both spoke to the convention that night to a rousing response. Later he gave me his contact information. I left the facility excited and appreciative of his generous spirit.

Over the next several years, we shared the stage at numerous events, and he was always gracious and helpful. I called him occasionally, and he received my calls as if I were the most important person who had ever contacted him. He had the gift of making each person feel special and, he certainly did that for me.

One day, soon after our first meeting, we were both scheduled to speak at an afternoon leadership conference. We were again alone in a room together, and I grabbed the opportunity to ask him several questions about what he had learned about leadership throughout his exceptional career.

He answered my questions thoughtfully. After a few minutes, I asked the question about which I was most curious. What did he think people needed most to learn if they wanted to become productive and successful leaders?

He first reminded me of the importance of goal setting. He told me that many intelligent and sincere men and women started careers and businesses without complete plans. They have a vague idea about what they want to do but often lack a detailed map to get there. He expressed his surprise at how many people he had met over the years reacted to life without clear goals. He believed that helping people identify and develop their goals was one of the most important things he had contributed. Then he paused and said that, even with goals and plans, one more thing was necessary if people wanted to fulfill their potential and rise as far as possible. He said that a person needed to have a sense of purpose to, as he put it, "reach the top."

He then told me how he had made the mistake of spending years pursuing success instead of purpose. He eventually realized that he had lived his life in reverse. He explained that when he changed his focus to finding and fulfilling his purpose rather than just trying to achieve success and create income, his entire life changed. This famous and influential man had found the secret of true achievement. Success is not your purpose; fulfilling your purpose is your success.

He then told me a personal story. He said that for part of his adult life, he was driven by selfishness and greed. He believed that he could only be happy if he became "rich and famous." But the more he pursued these twin "goals," the more unhappy and frustrated he became. Then he made a sincere and deep commitment to Christ and discovered his purpose. To his surprise, he changed from his determined drive to get things for himself and started to focus on how to help other people reach their dreams and accomplish their goals. He became a "giver." He found his purpose in serving others.

His income exploded, and eventually, he was giving away more money than he had previously made. His family noticed that he was happier than he had ever been. His success did not lead to his purpose; his purpose led to his success. At this point, he repeated a phrase that I had heard him use in his speeches. He said, "if you help enough people get what they need, you will get everything you need." I will always be grateful that Zig Ziglar took the time to invest in me in my early years as a motivational/ personal development speaker. He was generous and practical. He was kind to a "beginner."

Zig shared with me numerous techniques and tips and encouraged me on my path, but the most valuable input was his reminder of the power of purpose. The discovery of your purpose changes everything.

Watch Out for the Quicksand

You may have seen movies where an unwary individual accidentally walks into quicksand and becomes stuck. In the 1960s, by one estimate, around 3% of all films contained a scene of someone stuck in quicksand. The idea of the danger of quicksand is still a part of popular culture. You are not in a movie but may still be stuck in a "quicksand" of routine and lack of imagination and fail to see your purpose.

Many people enter their twenties eager to create income, start families, and build a better life. Often, they realize that life is harder than they expected, and it is easier to focus on surviving rather than thriving. Many individuals give up on their "dreams" and lower their expectations. They become stuck in "quicksand" and never move forward. This "quicksand syndrome" follows a predictable pattern.

Discouragement

When you realize that life is full of challenges and detours that keep you from your dreams, you can easily become discouraged. This happens when your time and energy are diverted into maintaining rather than growing your life.

This does not mean that it is wrong to work hard to pay your bills and complete your commitments. But you do not want your whole life dominated by the need to "just get by." I know that many of you are looking for a way to move out of the darkness of your discouragement and into the sunlight of success and freedom. You do not want to stay stuck in "quicksand." This book is designed to help you stay out of the "quicksand" and fulfill your life purpose.

The Disappointed Man

I met Brett at an event in Massachusetts. He was 28 and a college graduate. He had been married for three years and had recently bought a condo. He was tall and athletic with a pleasant personality. He made $65,000 a year analyzing data for an insurance company. He was also discouraged.

His discouragement was rooted in the postponement of his deepest desire. He had planned to attend Law School but had suspended his goal to get married and pay for his new condo. He was happy in his marriage (although it was more demanding than he had expected) and liked his condo, but his original dream seemed to be fading each year. He was afraid that he would never escape from his current situation. He was in "quicksand."

When I asked Brett about his purpose, he talked about paying off his condo and eventually having children. I said that although paying off his condo and having children were worthy goals, they were not a purpose. He looked surprised and asked me what I meant. I explained that his purpose was a mission he was meant to accomplish. It was what he wanted to be remembered for. It was something that made his life matter.

Brett started to cry. He was six feet four inches tall and built like a linebacker on an American football team, and he cried hard and long. When he stopped, he looked at me and said, "can you help me? I don't want to live my life and miss my purpose."

I asked him what he cared about outside of himself. He said that, as a child, he had imagined himself as a champion of people in need, who could not help themselves. His uncle was a lawyer, and he saw the Law profession as a pathway to protect people.

As we spoke, he realized that his purpose was not to be a lawyer or to make money; it was to defend people who needed a champion. His feelings of discouragement were a warning that he was missing his purpose. I saw Brett four years later at a conference in Phoenix, Arizona. He was a recent Law School graduate, still happily married, with a young son. He beamed with happiness and satisfaction. He told me that he had launched the career that he believed would complete his purpose.

Disappointment

The second sign that you are stuck in "quicksand" is an undercurrent of emotional disappointment. If you only concentrate on money and success, you will be disappointed. Often you get what you think you want and find it does not provide the satisfaction you anticipated. You are disappointed.

The Cake Batter Problem

When I was fourteen years old, I had a memorable experience with disappointment. I had developed a "sweet tooth" early in life as I helped in my grandmother's restaurant. The restaurant was a popular destination in our small town for over thirty years. I helped as a child and was "paid" with my selection of desserts and sweets. I started a lifelong love of milkshakes while working in the restaurant and still have a passion for cakes, candy, and pies.

My mother made a home-made cake every week, and I especially enjoyed scraping the batter from the bowl after she had transferred the contents to cake pans before placing them in the oven. One summer Saturday, my mother mixed her recipe in a bowl and poured the contents into the containers as usual. She and my dad had to be away for a couple of hours, and she left the pans filled with batter in the refrigerator.

After they left, I had what I thought was a brilliant idea. I used my mother's cake recipe to fill a bowl with cake batter. I then ate the entire bowl. I was congratulating myself on the abundance of cake batter I had consumed when I noticed a strange sensation in my stomach. In minutes I was rolling on the floor in agony. I had failed to consider the effect of one of the basic ingredients of cake batter: baking powder.

According to Wikipedia, "Baking powder is used to increase the volume and lighten the texture of baked goods. It works by releasing carbon dioxide gas into a batter or dough through an acid-base reaction, causing bubbles in the wet mixture to expand and thus leavening the mixture." In my desire to go beyond "licking the bowl" to eating all the cake batter I could hold; I had unintentionally created a crisis. *The* baking powder did what it was supposed to do and released carbon dioxide gas that caused the mixture to expand INSIDE.

MY STOMACH. I had done something stupid. I got what I wanted but did not receive the satisfaction I had hoped for. I was disappointed.

This is what happens when you lower your sights to aim only at money and success. Alone, they do not have the power to make you happy, but when they are connected to a greater purpose, they become supports for a bigger and better life. The ingredients in cake batter are there to make a cake, not fill a teenager's stomach. Money and success supposed to help you accomplish your purpose; they are not meant to be your main goals. I am not saying that it is wrong to be successful or bad to make money. I am saying that they are a means and not an end. You need something more and that "something more" is your mission. I enjoyed the cake batter at first, but I quickly learned that I could not live on cake batter alone. In the same way, you cannot live on money and success alone.

Doubt

When you experience disappointment and struggle with discouragement, you eventually sink deeper into the quicksand of doubt. You begin to doubt that your deeper dreams will ever come true, and you may even doubt whether you should have those dreams at all. Doubts rob you of energy and motivation and weaken your ability to pursue your goals. It is a well-established fact that confidence is vital for success. Doubt undermines your confidence and leaves you uncertain about your ability to create accomplishment. Doubt first grips you when you feel overwhelmed by the demands of life. Doubt is the beginning of fear, the fear that you may stay stuck where you are for the rest of your life.

The Young Man Who Doubted His Own Business

Carlos hosted me at a marketing conference in St. Louis, Missouri. Carlos was selected to take me to the auditorium to speak then return me to my hotel. He was 27 years old and full of life and excitement. I liked him immediately.

After I finished my presentation, Carlos escorted me to the hotel. We exited the convention center and followed a back street to the hotel entrance. It was a beautiful June morning, and he and I were alone on the street. When we reached the hotel door, Carlos stopped and asked if

I would answer a question.

Carlos explained that he had started his business three years before and had given it sincere commitment and effort. He believed in his opportunity and trusted the organization with which he was affiliated. He was part of an effective team. But even with all of this, he felt that something was wrong.

When I asked him to give me a review of his business development, it quickly became obvious that the slow growth of his business has caused him to doubt his ultimate success. His business had started with a surge of growth but had slowed to a trickle. Numerous difficulties had taken his energy and diverted his attention. His discouragement had produced his doubt.

I asked him if he still believed that his business model could lead him to the fulfillment of his goals, and he said yes. I then asked if he was still willing to trust his team, and he, again, said yes. By this time, I had realized the nature of his challenge. He had launched his business with sincere enthusiasm but had not considered the possibility of setbacks and obstacles. When the inevitable challenges arrived, he was not emotionally prepared to face them. I encouraged him to reconnect with his dreams and eliminate his doubt. The next time I saw him, his business was soaring into success.

The Woman Who Swam into History

Gertrude Ederle was an internationally acclaimed swimmer. She was intensely competitive and wanted to do something no woman had done in her sport. She decided to swim the English Channel, from the coast of Great Britain to the shores of France.

The English Channel is a part of the Atlantic Ocean that separates England from France. The first man to swim the Channel, Englishman Matthew Webb, chose the shortest route of around 22.5 miles (from

Dover to Calais). He entered the water on the English side on August 24, 1875, and walked out of the ocean on the French shore on August 25. It had taken him 21 hours and 45 minutes of immense effort.

In 1926, aware that no woman had matched Webb's feat, Gertrude decided to try the crossing herself. The American swimmer was already famous as an Olympic champion and had set world- record times in five events.

Although she was only five feet and five inches tall, she was a powerful swimmer, known popularly as the "Queen of the Waves." In 1925, according to her nephew, Bob, she "warmed up" for the attempt on the Channel by conducting what he called, "a midnight frolic" by swimming in the middle of the night 22 miles from Battery Park in New York City to Sandy Hook, New Jersey. Her record time of 7 hours and 11 minutes stood for 81 years until it was broken by an Australian swimmer, Tammy van Wisse, in 2006. Gertrude, who was known to her friends as Trudy, began training for her channel attempt shortly after her successful swim between Battery Park and Sandy Hook.

She decided that she needed help but disagreed with her first coach and chose to find someone else. She eventually settled on competitive swimming instructor, Bill Burgess, who had himself swum the Channel in 1911. With total commitment, she trained with Burgess until she felt ready for the challenge. Two of the serious risk factors that made the swim so dangerous were the water temperature, approximately 63 degrees.

Fahrenheit, well below the human body's core temperature, and the unpredictable currents that could add as much as 20- 30 miles to the swim.

Gertrude decided to reverse many previous routes and left from Cape Gris-Nez in France at 7:08 on the morning of August 6, 1926. Her only special equipment was a pair of motorcycle goggles she had lined with water-proof paraffin.

When she exited the water 14 hours and 34 minutes later, she had not only made a successful crossing, but she had also established a new record time for men and women. The previous record was 16 hours and 33 minutes set by Enrique Tiraboschi.

As Gertrude walked up the beach, she was met by a British immigration official who asked the "bleary-eyed, waterlogged teenager" (she was 20) for her passport.

When she returned to the United States, she was celebrated by two million people at a ticker-tape parade in her honor in Manhattan. She met Calvin Coolidge, the President of the United States, and traveled America giving speeches and swimming demonstrations. She died at 98 in Wyckoff, New Jersey, after a full and remarkable life.

There is one more critical element in Gertrude's story. It is the most crucial detail of the entire account, and I have saved it for last.

One brief, solitary moment almost stole Gertrude's eventual success and could have cost her, her life. After several hours of swimming in the cold, gray waters of the Atlantic, she entered what competitive distance swimmers call "the death zone." You enter the "death zone" when the excitement at the start and the adrenaline at the beginning have faded, and tiredness and boredom capture the swimmer. Alone in the water (although there is always a small boat nearby), the swimmer faces a drop in determination that often leads to a feeling of depression and even despair. This "death zone" usually occurs in the approximate middle of the route when the swimmer realizes how much distance remains to the end.

This is the point when some competitors wave at the emergency boat and ask to be removed from the water. The "death zone" is so named not just because of the possibility of physical death but because of the "death" of the dream as well. When Gertrude entered the "death zone" she faced the most critical decision of her experience. She could let her dream die or decide to continue toward her goal. Gertrude decided to keep swimming, and all her later success came because of that decision. The secret of surviving the "death zone" is to continue until you pass through. Competitive distance swimmers claim that once you decide to plow through the "zone," your strength is renewed, and your energy restored. You move from the doubt of the "death zone" into a recovered belief in your dream.

This is what Winston Churchill meant when he urged the British nation to persist in the fight against Nazi tyranny. This is the reason he repeatedly said to "never, never, never give up."

A Stressful Moment over the Pacific Ocean

I was flying to Australia to speak. I had found it difficult to leave Amy and our family for two weeks. I had just finished a crowded speaking schedule and was tired and depleted.

I flew to Los Angeles, waited two hours in the airport, then boarded the 20-hour flight to Sydney. Somewhere over the Pacific Ocean, I awoke from a nap. The plane was dark and quiet. I sat up and looked at the sleeping passengers all around me and suddenly felt a wave of disorientation and depression. I doubted my decision to accept the Australian speaking tour and doubted my ability to fulfill my responsibilities. I was sure I had made a terrible mistake.

Then I remembered the story of Gertrude Ederle and the "death zone" she encountered somewhere in the windswept waters of the English Channel. I realized that I had entered a small "death zone" of my own. Because I was tired and in an unfamiliar environment, my emotions were dominated by doubt. As I thought of Gertrude, I pushed through my "death zone." I prayed for strength and renewed my commitment to help the people I would be speaking to in Australia. I eventually had one of the most powerful and influential experiences of my life during my two-week visit.

Doubt comes when difficulties and challenges threaten your direction. Doubt slows you down and saps your strength. Doubt replaces your confidence and smashes your motivation. Doubt pulls you into the "death zone." But remember that you are not doomed to defeat in the "death zone." You can choose to keep swimming until you reach the other shore.

Default

When something moves to its "default" position, it returns to something that was pre-programmed to produce an automatic response. The default settings on your computer were put there by someone else.

Life decisions are not always based on a sense of purpose. Instead, they may be founded on a default position that was programmed into you by another person. Sometimes you find that you are fulfilling someone else's dreams instead of your own. This does not mean that you should ignore the input of the individuals who are a part of your life. Guidance from parents, teachers, and mentors provides valuable content to your choices. One part of wisdom is to carefully consider the contributions of people who care about you. You can make disastrous decisions when you are too stubborn to listen to direction. You should always respect wise counsel.

But sometimes, the information you receive may not form the right foundation for you. Your mission is your unique calling, and, when you retreat to the "default" position you were programmed to accept, then you may miss your mission.

The Poor Boy from Mississippi

One of the most respected professors in my graduate school told me that his greatest struggle had been to change from the direction some early influences wanted him to follow and find the path that was best for him. He grew up in a disadvantaged family in rural Mississippi with little opportunity for education and advancement. He became a Christian when a young man and soon became active in his local church. His parents were busy trying to create income from a small farm, and he became dependent on several church members for guidance and support.

One day, a man who wanted to help him, took him aside and told him that, in his opinion, the young man had limited intellectual capacity and should plan to farm like his parents.

The professor who told me the story said that he was shocked and discouraged. He had felt the faint beginning of a spark of desire for a better life and interpreted the older man's words as an effort to extinguish that spark. He tried to tell the man that he had sensed the stirring of desire to serve God and help people and wanted to pursue education to do both. The man would not listen and insisted that the young man accept his place in life as a rural farmer.

For two years, this young man wrestled with his choices. He debated whether to return to his "default" setting or to resist that easy path and attempt to rise from his circumstances.

Eventually his sense of purpose won and, he worked and saved money until he was able to enter college. He graduated from college, earned a doctorate and, became a professor at a respected graduate school where I became one of his students. When this professor was a young man, he was deeply imprinted by the expectations of someone else. Those outside expectations became his default position and almost kept him from his purpose. This is a critical lesson for everyone. You need to discover your mission not, the mission of someone else.

Distress

Distress starts when you recognize that the path you are traveling may not get you to the destination you want. Stress is a part of the word distress for a good reason. Distress is simply another form of stress and anxiety. Distress is also rooted in fear. Fear may cause you to turn off your "dream switch" and accept mediocrity. Fear keeps you from your possibilities and squeezes out your energy. Do not allow fear and distress to determine your decisions.

Division

If you stay in the quicksand long enough, you may start blaming other people for your unhappiness, which causes division. When your feelings of disappointment and discouragement take control, you begin to fire "blame bullets" at the closest targets. You "divide yourself" from those who could help you.

The Couple Who Argued Their Way into Failure

My wife and I once worked with a couple who started with big dreams but eventually descended into a pit of petty arguments. They began in the sunshine of love and excitement, but when the challenges came, they chose division over unity.

It started with the wife. She refused to face her shopping addiction and continually maxed out her credit cards while expecting her husband to pay the bills. They were struggling with serious debt, but when she received an unexpected inheritance, she spent the money on enhancements for her home instead of eliminating debt. As her spending increased, the pressure on her husband increased. Soon he was delaying his dreams to pay for her habit. He loved his wife and cared about her happiness, but the constant stress wore him down.

Amy and I arrived one evening to share dinner with this couple, and as we stood on the steps of their house, we heard the couple yelling and throwing insults at one another. We were unsure what to do but decided to see if we could help. I knocked on the door and waited. The argument stopped, and, after a few moments, the door opened. The husband stood in the entrance, embarrassed, and uncertain. He stared at us, then motioned us into the house.

I do not remember that evening for the food or the entertainment. I remember the evening as the breakthrough this couple urgently needed. After an awkward opening, we assured this couple of our concern and friendship. They relaxed, and we discussed their situation. They seemed eager to share their challenge with someone they trusted. As we spoke, they realized that, in their distress, they had divided from one another. They apologized to each other and us and even occasionally laughed about their situation.

One of the revealing insights that surfaced in the conversation came from the memory of their early years together. They recalled that, as Christians, they wanted to honor God together and had pictured a life of generosity and service. They cared about people and had often given time to contribute to the needs of others. When I asked what had pushed them off their path, the wife responded with honesty and clarity; she said that she had always felt inferior as a child and had been often embarrassed by the financial condition of her parents. These childhood disappointments caused her to create strategies to prove to herself and others that she was a successful and worthy individual, which led to overactive shopping. Her excessive purchases were a way to "show the world" that she deserved respect.

Her husband was shocked by his wife's admissions. He had only seen the problems caused by her spending and never had suspected the root reasons of her choices. He responded with grace and compassion. It was clear that he wanted to bring healing and reassurance to his wife. The evening ended with prayer and a commitment to reorganize their finances and relaunch their marriage. It was a special night. This couple had made the mistake of substituting their unmet needs for their purpose, which caused them to allow their needs to consume them. It would have been better for this wife to meet her need for respect by doing good and fulfilling her original sense of purpose rather than by creating an artificial shopping system in the hope that it would heal her heart. The husband would have been more effective in solving his wife's problems by listening and understanding rather than by exploding with anger and blame. They remembered their mission and renewed their commitment to fulfill their purpose together rather than dividing from one another.

The Root Reminder

If you want to escape the quicksand and rise to your purpose, you need to practice the "root reminder" approach. The most influential mentor in my life told me that if you can discover the root of something, you can understand and deal with it effectively. This means that when you find the root, you can manage the fruit. The root of the wife's shopping addiction in the previous story was her sense of inferiority. The root of the husband's anger was his frustration at being unable to help the wife he loved. The root of the unhappiness the graduate school professor felt as a teenager was the wrong direction forced on him by someone else. The root of Gertrude Ederle's desire to swim the English Channel was to accomplish something no woman had done.

What is your "root"? What is your core reason for what you do or hope to do? Success is a vague and meaningless idea unless it has a purpose that defines it. If "success" is your goal, then it does not matter what you choose for your success. if it is "successful." Your success, then, is equally meaningful whether you become excellent at selling illegal weapons to criminals or building tree hospitals for children.

So, the real question is, "why do you want to be successful"? What is your "root" reason? But when asked what they want out of life, many people give fuzzy, unclear answers. They want to be:

- Famous

- Rich

- Happy

People often desire fame because they fear that they are unimportant without it. A frenzied involvement with social media can be your way to prove that you matter because you are "noticed." Facebook "likes" can seem like a validation of your existence. Posting on Instagram, Snapchat, or YouTube, make your thoughts and opinions available to people who "don't even know you," so you must be important. The pursuit of more social media "friends" becomes proof of your worth. The desire to be rich is, for many people, the desire to be free from fear. You think that if you have enough money, you will avoid concerns about food, shelter, medical care, or transportation. For other people, money represents the freedom to get what you want and to enjoy possessions and experiences. I heard a man in a store once remarking to his friend that if he could just purchase a 60-inch, flat-screen, high-definition television, he would be happy. That may have been true, at least, until he tired of the device and wanted the next technological edition of the TV.

The secret of money is to understand that it is only a means to something else. If your root desire is for your family to live in a safe and secure neighborhood, then you will need to earn the income to put them in a better place. If you desire to create a business that your children can inherit and develop, then you need to build a profitable business first. Do not just say you want to be "rich," identify the reason you want more money, and plan to earn the income to fulfill that dream. Find your "root" and then produce your "fruit." Almost everyone says they want to be happy. But there is a crucial difference between feeling good and the satisfaction of true happiness. I can enjoy the taste and sensual experience of a well-prepared meal but, that momentary encounter with quality food will not make my life happy. A passing experience is not the same as a lifetime of contentment and fulfillment.

Always remember three things about happiness.

First, happiness is based on actions that do good and improve life. Happiness is founded on the worthwhile things you do, not the occasional things you feel.

The second source of happiness is a continual spirit of service (it's not about you).
And the third is that your experience of happiness is based on the happiness you create for others.

The Amateur Funeral

When I was seventeen years old, I was asked to conduct a funeral. I was not an ordained minister and had no theological training. I had been speaking in several local churches and a family who had just lost a beloved mother, grandmother, and great-grandmother (the same person) had heard me speak and decided I should conduct the funeral.

I was, in many ways, a typical teenager. I liked pop music, thought girls were mysterious and intriguing, enjoyed playing basketball with my friends after school, and listening to the Cincinnati Reds baseball team and the Kentucky Wildcats basketball team on the radio. When the family asked me to do the funeral, I was scared but said yes. I did not want to disappoint them. I had met the woman who had died and remembered her as lively and funny. She was known for her warm Christian generosity. I knew enough about her to compose what I hoped would be a positive and affirming message.

The funeral was conducted in a small country church, surrounded by farms and mountains. It was a warm spring day, and flowers were blooming in abundance. Members of the woman's immediate and extended family crowded into the church, along with numerous friends. She had been well-liked. When I arrived at the church, I discovered that I was responsible for everything. I led the service, read the obituary, guided the music, and preached the sermon. At first, I felt overwhelmed, but when I saw the expectant faces of the family, I determined to do all I could to provide a meaningful service. I prayed for help (very sincerely!) and plunged in. I managed to complete the service without serious mistakes (I got the order wrong, but no one noticed, especially since I was the only one on the program).

When the funeral ended, I waited at the front until the audience filed by the casket and, the body was removed. I exited the church and walked to the front where the woman's son was waiting for me. He said, "well, are you ready"? I replied, "ready for what"? He looked puzzled then said, "are you ready for the graveside service"? In my inexperience, I did not know there would be a graveside service or that I would be doing it. I walked over to the funeral director and asked for the location of the gravesite. He told me that the casket would need to be carried up the side of a mountain to a private family cemetery on top of a ridge. It had rained earlier in the day, and the mountain slope was muddy and slippery. I had to help push and drag the casket up a 45-degree incline. I fell so often that I was quickly covered in mud and briers. Once I even lost my grip on the casket and watched the poor woman slide ten feet until a staff person from the funeral home managed to throw himself in front of the container and stop its descent. After almost thirty minutes of grunting effort, we reached the ridge. I looked at the simple grave awaiting us and saw on the side, the tear-stained faces of the woman's children and grandchildren who had climbed a trail to reach the site. The sun erupted from the clouds, and a warm breeze stirred the newly leafed trees. I quoted a few Bible verses, acknowledged the woman's Christian faith, and prayed. Then it was over. The family each thanked me and said it was precisely the service their loved one would have wanted. I found out that she had requested me for her service after one of my youthful sermons.

We followed the path down the mountain, and the family dispersed to their cars. I was left alone. I walked to my car and opened the door. My only suit was ruined, and it never recovered. No one paid me for my services (I had not expected anything). So much mud had covered my clothes that it took two hours to clean the seats of the car. I had used the time I needed to study for finals (I was about to graduate from High School), and I was exhausted. But when I entered and sat in the car something wonderful happened. I was suddenly flooded with pure joy. I had never felt "happier" in my life. This sense of happiness was not based on scoring the winning shot in a game or consuming my favorite dessert. It did not flow from an hour watching my favorite TV show or attending a popular movie. It came from my service to a hurting family that needed me. I had done something good for someone else, and the flood of joy was the result.

Happiness is a momentary, fleeting emotion that is caused by an immediate circumstance. Joy rises in your heart when you fulfill your purpose. So, the lesson is simple. Focus on your purpose first, and fulfillment will follow.

The next chapter is unusual. It contains personal stories that explain how I came to an understanding of my purpose. The stories that follow are from my life and experience. They are intended to illustrate the principles that lead to a sense of purpose. You may never have similar experiences and may not need them. Your purpose is yours and mine is mine. God works with everyone in ways that fit that person. The reason for the following chapter is to open a window into my life that will, hopefully, help you understand the power of purpose.

CHAPTER 3

Signals

Are you restless and often feel that you are searching for something? When you pause in your routine, is there a sense that you are missing a piece of your puzzle? Do you sometimes wake in the night with a pull toward something that you cannot name and do not understand? In your honest moments, are you aware of a nagging dissatisfaction with your life that makes you want something more? The reason for all of this may surprise you. The truth is that someone may be signaling you. Someone may be trying to get your attention, and your restless, searching feeling is a response to the signal.

The Early Morning Emergency

Several years ago, I was taking an early morning walk at our home in Fayetteville, Georgia (we have since moved to Kentucky). I rose before dawn, dressed, and traveled along a country road that connected our house with a series of small lakes. It was a misty Sunday morning in July, and the sun was just beginning to cut through the fog. July is blisteringly hot in Georgia, and I had chosen my pre-dawn start to avoid the rising temperature. I was enjoying the soft breeze and the surrounding birdsong. I walked to the edge of the second lake, turned around, and started back. Soon I topped a small hill near our property and saw our house at the bottom.

When I had left for my walk, Amy and our daughter Allison were still asleep, and the house was dark. When I returned, the sun was not yet fully risen. The streetlights were still burning, and mist curled around the trees. But one thing was dramatically different. Every light in the house was blazing. Lights shone from every window in every room. The outside lights on our front porch were all on. Even the lights on our back deck were broadcasting into the early morning mist. The house seemed strikingly alive.

I stopped on the crest of the hill and wondered why such a display of light had replaced the darkened house I had left an hour before. Then I realized the meaning of the moment. It was a signal. Amy was trying to alert me to something important. Thinking she or Allison might be hurt, I ran the rest of the distance to the house. When I reached the edge of the home, Amy was waiting for me on the porch. I jumped up the porch steps and asked her if anything was wrong. She said that everything was fine and explained that she had been awakened by an urgent phone call. I had been the special preaching assistant to Dr. Charles Stanley, senior pastor of the First Baptist Church of Atlanta for the previous three years, and I was "on-call" for whenever he needed me. When I returned the call to Dr. Stanleys assistant, she said that Dr. Stanley was sick, and he wanted me to fill in for him that morning. It was the Fourth of July, and the church was expecting thousands of people for the largest service of the year. I told the assistant that I would be there as soon as possible. I spoke that morning on a theme I had been developing for several weeks. The message was entitled *The Moral Map of America*. The response was intense and enthusiastic.

A Meeting with the Vice President

A few months later, I received a call from Dr. Stanley asking me to meet with then-Vice President George H. W. Bush. President Ronald Reagan was finishing his second term, and Bush was organizing his campaign for the presidency. Bush was coming to Atlanta to meet with evangelical Christian leaders to discuss his campaign, and Dr. Stanley asked me to attend the meeting.

After being cleared by the Secret Service, I arrived at the private entrance of a downtown Atlanta hotel. I was escorted to an upper floor, brought to a room, and told to wait. After a few minutes, two men entered the room. Both were prominent pastors in metro Atlanta. We introduced ourselves and took our seats. Soon the door opened again, and a man announced Vice President Bush. Mr. Bush entered the room, warmly greeted each of us, and thanked us for coming. We then spent two hours discussing Mr. Bush's campaign and his policy positions. The three of us asked Mr. Bush about his faith and beliefs. He responded graciously and honestly. I was especially impressed with his references to his Christian mother. He was close to his mother and had been powerfully influenced by her spiritual example.

When the meeting ended, a White House photographer took pictures, and the other two men left. I lingered and asked if I could accompany the Vice President to the elevator. He agreed, and the two of us walked down the hallway. We were almost to the elevator when I asked Mr. Bush if I could give him an audio recording of the message, I had done the previous Fourth of July, The Moral Map of America. He graciously accepted, and I gave him an audio of the sermon. One month later, I received two messages. The first was a handwritten note from the Vice President thanking me for the recording, along with comments about specific points he had liked (which meant he had listened to it). The second was a request from a White House official asking if I would like to become a speechwriter for the Vice President (I declined because I was happily on another track).

George H. W. Bush was elected president and I noticed that several of Bush's campaign and policy speeches made specific references to positions we had encouraged him to consider. He even used some of the same words and phrases we had shared with him. This process started with the signal I had received on my early morning walk on the fourth of July the previous year.

I believe that the signals you receive are necessary. They matter. You are receiving signals for a reason. Certain things will only happen if you respond to the signal. I know that some of you who are reading this do not share my Christian faith and worldview. I understand that. But I hope you will continue to read for three reasons.

First, whether I am right or wrong about the source of the signal, you still need to be alert to whatever can give you accurate direction. Secular and religious people both sense something that pulls them forward. Some call this source God, and some call it "Destiny" (I firmly believe it is God).

The Greatest Communicator of the Nineteenth Century

Young Charles Spurgeon believed he heard God's voice signaling him at a crucial life point. Spurgeon was a nineteenth-century British Baptist preacher who is still the most widely read Christian communicator in history. His works have been read more than any other Christian teacher and are still studied today. His published sermons contain 25 million words and are the equivalent of the entire 27 volume Ninth Edition of the *Encyclopedia Britannica*.

When Spurgeon was in his teens, he was invited to meet the head of a college he hoped to attend. A servant placed him in the wrong room of the house where the meeting was to take place, and the leader of the college left, thinking Spurgeon was uninterested. When Spurgeon learned of the mistake, he was crushed. Spurgeon was from a poor family (he was one of 17 children), and college in that time was only for a tiny minority of the population. He left the house convinced that he had missed the opportunity of a lifetime.

As he walked across Hyde Park, in London, he decided to ask for another meeting with the head of the college in hopes that his dream could be reborn. As he remembered years later, he was almost at the end of the park when he heard what he described as an "inner voice." That voice told him not to reapply but to pursue a pastoral ministry instead. Spurgeon later recalled the specific words of this "inner voice." The voice quoted a verse from the Bible in Jeremiah 45:5, *"Should you then seek great things for yourself? Seek them not"* For the rest of his life, Spurgeon believed that his "inner voice" was from God.

Spurgeon's dynamic career might have been far different if he had followed a traditional college route (this is not a criticism of higher education, which is the right choice for many people). Spurgeon's decision to listen to "the signal" led him to develop a unique, individualized style that set him apart from every other Christian communicator in his generation. By the time he was 20, he had prepared and preached over 600 sermons and had discovered an ability to explain the Bible that has rarely been matched, even in our time. His insights and "out of the box" methods continue to influence leaders over a hundred and twenty- five years after his death. When he died, he was the most read author in the world. Spurgeon became the most widely read and influential Christian leader of the nineteenth century because he listened to his "signal."

Following Destiny

Two of the most revealing examples of secular people following their "signal" are Napoleon and Winston Churchill. Napoleon wrote and frequently spoke of following his "Destiny." Napoleon wrote, "Destiny urges me to a goal of which I am ignorant. Until that goal is attained, I am invulnerable, unassailable. When Destiny has accomplished her purpose in me, a fly may suffice to destroy me." Churchill had a similar view of his destiny and purpose. In his memoirs, Churchill wrote of his appointment as Prime minister of Great Britain at the beginning of the Second World War, "I felt as if I were walking with destiny, and that all my past life had been but a preparation for this hour and for this trial...I thought I knew a good deal about it all. I was sure I should not fail". The man many historians think is the greatest of all the American Presidents, Abraham Lincoln, felt a similar sense of purpose. He blended his sense of purpose with spiritual understanding. He famously said, "My concern is not whether God is on our side; my greatest concern is to be on God's side, for God is always right."

Each of these examples has a common theme. Each individual listed was being signaled to do something that mattered, and their response to the signal determined their future. This is the reason why careful goal setting is so important. When you align your goals with your purpose, miracles can happen.

The second reason you should continue reading is that I may be right. It is always possible that God is the one signaling you, and your purpose depends on your proper reception of the signal. That makes you incredibly special.

The third reason you should keep reading is simple. The techniques and procedures you can use to find your mission are transferable to every part of your life. Whether you share my beliefs or not, these techniques and methodologies can still help you. When I relay stories about how Gods signals work in my own life and how they have influenced me, I request that you have an open mind and learn the practical lessons that these stories contain. My purpose in this book is to help you find your mission. I hope to help you understand and correctly interpret the signals you receive every day. Some of you may think that your signals are your sub-conscious ideas trying to get your attention while others may agree with me that God is sending the signals. But if you care about finding your purpose, then you still must learn to translate the signals successfully.

There have been several key moments in my life when my choices were guided by the right signals. I want you to experience some of these moments so you can better understand why I believe what I believe as well as understand why it is so vital that you hear your signals when they come.

The Surprise Election

When I was fifteen years old, I was selected by my church to be a delegate at the state-wide summer conference of all United Methodist church youth groups in Kentucky. The meeting was a significant event with high school students attending from different regions of the state. I arrived at the college that was hosting the conference and was escorted to an orientation session. There were hundreds of students who were all excited about the opportunity to meet, learn, and grow. I quickly became friends with several students and began to relax and enjoy the sessions. For the next few days, I participated in a whirlwind of activities, classes, and chapels. My friend base steadily expanded, and I was swept up in the fun and personal development of the week.

I was intrigued to find that many of the students had serious spiritual questions and were eager to discuss the Bible and how its teachings applied to our lives. By the second day, I was meeting with over two hundred students and leading discussions on spiritual subjects. I had no training other than my study of the Bible and my deep desire to know more about God. I did not understand why so many students wanted my input, but I was happy to give what limited guidance I could.

The last full day of the conference, we assembled in a large hall and were told that we were supposed to elect the officers who would lead all the youth groups in the state for the coming year. We were instructed to write nominations and submit them. The nominations would then be announced later in the day and be voted on at the final session. When the session ended, I left with a group to eat lunch. After the meal, I was walking back to my dorm room when two students intercepted me. A young woman said that she and her companion were there to notify me that I had been nominated to be the state-wide president for all youth groups for the coming year. She congratulated me then added her view that I probably would not win because the other nominee was a young man who had been coming to the conference for two years, was well-known and was also the current vice-president. Everyone, she said, expected him to win (including her). She continued that it was an honor to be nominated and that I should not feel bad when I lost. She wished me well, and they both left.

As I proceeded to my room, I tried to process what I was told. It had never occurred to me that I might be nominated for any of the state offices. I was in my first year and one of the youngest delegates (I was fifteen). I had only known the other students for a few days. As I walked, I decided to decline the nomination. I had no experience leading an organization and was nervous and uncertain about the possibility I knew the current vice-president and had been impressed with his confidence. He and I had even publicly debated some points that arose in the informal gatherings where all the students shared and mingled. I fully expected him to win. I entered my dorm room and suddenly became aware of something different. I had an overwhelming feeling that I should accept the nomination. I had no sense of the outcome of the election, just a sense that I should not withdraw. I knelt my bed and prayed for guidance. When I finished, I felt a wave of calm and peace. We voted by secret ballot during the final session of the day. No results were immediately available, and I left with some friends to walk to the campus cafeteria. While we were walking, I saw one of the out-going state officers hurrying towards us. We turned as a group, and he stopped and informed me that I had just been elected as the president of the state organization. I had won by one vote. To say that I was surprised would be an understatement. I was shocked because I had never expected to win. I went on to serve as state president the following year. I spoke in numerous churches and represented the state in national denominational affairs. I was introduced to the college where I later received my training and met my wife. I met church and business leaders throughout the state who became friends and supporters. The entire trajectory of my life was changed.

Why does this story matter? Because it was my first encounter with a "signal." When I decided to withdraw my name from the nomination and returned to my dorm room, I was stopped by a signal. When I listened to the signal, I knew that I was supposed to accept the nomination. I still believed I would not win, but the signal led me to stay in the game. The reason I told you that story is so that you can understand the importance of aligning your life with your true purpose. I do not know your purpose, but I do believe that your happiness and satisfaction in life depends on your discovery of that purpose. That is why you need to pay attention to the signals you sense. I am not saying that all of life is led by mysterious, mystical forces that appear and disappear as you need them. What I am saying is that almost everyone has moments of intuition and insight that can clarify your direction. Those moments are filled with signals.

Have you ever faced a decision that left you uneasy? Have you ever made a financial commitment that carried an unshakeable sense of doubt? Have you ever worked with someone who seemed to have all the ingredients of a right relationship but caused you a nagging concern? These feelings of unease, doubt, and anxiety may be the signals that could save you from a wrong choice or a bad relationship.

The Wrong Woman

When I was a senior in college, I met a young woman who had transferred to our school in the middle of the year. We became friends and began to date. She was attractive and fun, and the relationship quickly deepened. One evening I escorted her to her dorm following a dinner date. We were late returning and had to report to the woman who was responsible for the dorm to gain access (it was a private Christian liberal arts college with strict social rules and curfews). We both knew the older woman who administered the dorm and engaged her in conversation. I mentioned that I had an announcement to make (I was about to inform her that I would be attending summer school to finish my degree). She interrupted me with a giant grin and said that she already knew the nature of my announcement. She said that I was about to tell her that the young woman and I were getting married. I was startled, and for reasons, I still do not understand, heard myself saying, "yes, we are getting married." The young woman with me looked surprised, then said, "yes, we are getting married."

I left both the young woman and the dorm administrator, and returned to my dorm, amazed that I was unexpectedly engaged. For the next several weeks, the "engagement" gathered momentum. Word of our impending marriage had quickly spread through our campus. I soon found myself with an engagement ring and a deposit on a place to live. I traveled to another state to meet her parents, and she accompanied me to eastern Kentucky to meet my mom and dad. We planned for the wedding, bought a dress, and selected a date in August. As events moved at a blurring speed, I began to sense a tiny but persistent doubt. At first, I ignored this doubt. I did not want to disappoint either the young woman or the people who were involved in this "runaway train" I was riding. It was now mid-April, and I was on an almost empty campus one weekend. My "fiancée" was visiting her parents, and I was working on class requirements before my graduation in May. It was mid-afternoon, and I was hungry, so I went to the cafeteria. I entered and noticed a woman student sitting at a table talking with two male students. I had a casual, surface acquaintance with the young woman who was two years younger than me. She was pretty and popular and was known as being both great fun and deeply spiritual. I had thought once about dating her when she first arrived as a freshman but had decided against it when I realized how many other young men were asking her out (22 young men were ahead of me that month).

As I stood in line, deciding what to eat, something unexpected happened. With no warning, I was suddenly flooded with powerful emotions. I looked at the young woman sitting over thirty yards away and, although I barely knew her, I was overcome with an undeniable wish that I was marrying her instead of the young woman to whom I was engaged. I was so swept away by the surprise emotion that forgot my hunger and left the cafeteria. The rest of this story is in my book How to Have a Great Marriage, but I will give you a summary of what happened.

I ended the engagement two weeks later (with sincere apologies to the young woman and her parents, it was not her fault) and graduated without again seeing the young woman in the cafeteria.

I returned for summer school to finish my foreign language requirement. I drove onto campus at five o'clock on a warm June morning. I had to mail a check and walked to a campus mailbox. As I approached the mailbox, I had one of the most magical moments of my life. Like in a scene from a movie, I watched as a shaft of sunlight broke through the early morning mist and suddenly illuminated a young woman who, a moment before, had been hidden in the swirling fog. It was the young woman from the cafeteria. By the end of the month, we were dating. By October, I knew I wanted to be with her for the rest of my life. By the next year, we were married. I have been (and remain) wildly happy with the woman God selected for me. She is the perfect partner for my life and has been vital to everything I have accomplished. I love her more passionately now than ever. My life has been awesomely blessed because I received a surprise signal one April afternoon in a college cafeteria and responded to that signal.

The Surprise in the Snow

Not every signal is a warning to change direction. Some signals are guides to more significant opportunities.

When I was in graduate school at Emory University in Georgia, I went through a period of intense doubt. I had received a scholarship to attend the doctoral program at the university and an offer to teach in another graduate school when I completed my degree. But, as my program progressed, I developed an uneasiness I could not escape. I became uncertain about my direction and prayed for guidance. During Christmas break, I was invited to attend a retreat at the historic Shaker Village in

Kentucky with the other recipients of the scholarship. Those of us who were selected for the program were at different universities. We were all pursuing doctorates, and the retreat was an opportunity for us to spend time together and compare our experiences.

I arrived at the Lexington, Kentucky airport and was picked up by a driver who took me the site. Shaker Village is a restored nineteenth property composed of beautiful buildings, erected by the Shaker religious group as a private community apart from the surrounding area. The first day was filled with seminars and discussions. I appreciated the meetings and learned valuable new information but still felt a restlessness within. I knew something was off but could not identify the problem.

That evening, after dinner I returned to my simple Shaker room, filled with furniture designed and built by Shaker craftsmen over a hundred years before. Everything about my involvement should have made me proud and happy. I was getting a degree at a respected university. My tuition and expenses were paid. I had a job offer when I finished. I was wildly happy with Amy, the young woman from the cafeteria I had married. And I was a special guest at a retreat hosted at a unique and charming location. But I was still uneasy.

I decided to go for a walk. It was December and very cold, so I bundled up and went outside. Shaker Village is crisscrossed by long, meandering paths, covered in hand-cut limestone, that curve around and among the historic buildings, and I followed one of these for almost an hour. As I walked, it began to snow. By the time I returned to my building, the snow had covered the ground, and large flakes swirled around my head. I was on the edge of the area where my building was located when I received "a signal." I suddenly became aware that I was in the wrong place, pursuing the wrong mission and would never be satisfied until I fulfilled the right mission. I was not supposed to be a professor; I was supposed to help people through speaking and writing without the restrictions of an academic position. I had assumed that the scholarship and acceptance at a well-known university were proof I was on the right path. I had jumped at the opportunity to launch a teaching career but had failed to listen to the signals that warned me of my misdirection. The restlessness and unease I felt were the signals that I was traveling in the wrong direction.

As I stood in the snow that December night, I felt an enormous weight lift and knew that I had to follow the signals back to my real prupose. When I returned to Atlanta, I told Amy what had happened (she was not surprised), resigned my scholarship, and withdrew from the program. I had never felt such total peace and joy.

The Miracle in the Mailbox

While I was in the degree program, I was also working at a large downtown Atlanta church as a program director for outreach to college and university students in the Atlanta metro area. I was busy coordinating activities during the Christmas break and looked forward to a few days off between Christmas day and New Year's Eve. The day after Christmas, I received an invitation to attend a motivational conference in Ft. Lauderdale, Florida. Amy and I thought Florida was an excellent destination in December and were eager to experience our first motivational meeting but had no money to attend. The cost of the conference, including travel and expenses, came to exactly $300.00. Amy and I had a strong feeling that we should go but could not afford to make it happen.

One evening I went to the church to pick up some papers. It was a large, complex building, and I had to go through the section with staff mailboxes to reach my small office. I rarely received mail (everything went to our apartment) but decided to open my inbox. When I swung the small door open, I saw an envelope within. Curious, I opened the envelope and was amazed to find three one-hundred-dollar bills. An accompanying note said that the giver had "felt led" to place the money in my mailbox. I returned to our apartment and told Amy about the "miracle in the mailbox." She and I made immediate plans to drive to Ft. Lauderdale and attend the conference. The conference was everything we had expected, bur one specific element of the meeting was the reason we had been "signaled" to go. We were supposed to hear a speaker who inspired an idea that eventually led me to a further understanding of my purpose.

We had heard of Dr. Robert Schuller and were excited to find him on the program. The night he spoke, I expected a traditional sermon but instead listened to a dynamic motivational message with sermon elements. What I heard was a new communication approach (at least for me), and I was intrigued at how Dr. Schuller combined the Bible with positive success training. I had never heard the Bible applied to life in such a practical way. I was inspired. We returned to Atlanta filled with enthusiasm for the future and walked into another signal we never saw coming.

The Explosion on the Balcony

While I had been engaged in the doctoral program at Emory University and working on the staff of the church, I noticed an increasing buzz about a remarkable pastor who was stirring up the city.

Dr. Charles Stanley was the senior pastor of the First Baptist Church and had just launched a local television program. Amy and I had watched his show was impressed with his exceptional knowledge of the Bible and his ability to communicate. We had visited his church for a music concert but had never heard him personally. On a Saturday morning, I was walking to my car in the apartment parking lot and suddenly felt that I should attend Dr. Stanley's church the next morning. I told Amy, and she agreed. We arrived at the church fifteen minutes before the service and found parking with difficulty. Almost three thousand people were already in the auditorium, and we finally found seats in a balcony on the side of the sanctuary. We settled in as the service began.

When Dr. Stanley stood to speak, we were captivated by his message. He gave exceptional insights and told stories that touched our hearts. He was nearing the end when an explosion of emotion rocked me. I was instantly aware that I was supposed to do something important. I mentally moved away from the message and focused on the signal I was receiving. I suddenly felt a great calm and knew that I was supposed to speak with Dr. Stanley personally. I had no idea how to make this happen but remained open. The service concluded, and Amy and I stood to leave. The balcony was as crowded as the main floor, and we had to wait several minutes before we could walk toward the downstairs exit. By the time we reached the stairs, we were the last ones on the balcony. Because we were unfamiliar with the building, we were confused about how to find the hallway we had entered. Amy and I finally chose a door and passed through. There standing alone was Dr. Stanley.

I later learned that Dr. Stanley had never used that exit and (except for that morning) was never without an assistant. But there he was alone and standing at the door through which we had exited. I introduced Amy and myself. Then before Dr. Stanley could reply, I blurted out that I was a graduate student and church youth coordinator and was facing the greatest crisis of my life. I told him I had been praying for direction and asked if I could talk with him. He looked thoughtful and asked if I could be at his office the next morning at 11 o'clock. I said, yes. I later learned that he was booked for appointments for three months with no openings, but he had made one for me.

I arrived early and waited. At precisely 11 o'clock, an assistant escorted me into his office. Dr. Stanley greeted me and offered me a seat. He sat down opposite me and told me that he was meeting me because he sensed the need to do so (a signal). He asked me to explain my "crisis." I told him about the doctoral program, the offered professorship, and my job at the church.

I finished and told Dr. Stanley that I knew God had a mission for me, and I wanted to find it. He told me that his grandfather had once given him one of the most crucial pieces of advice he had ever received. His grandfather reminded him that the most important thing young Charles Stanley would ever do was to obey God and fulfill His purpose. He added that his grandfather had used a graphic image to drive the point home. He had told his grandson, "Charlie, if God tells you to go through a brick wall, you head for the wall and let God do the rest." Dr. Stanley then looked at me intently and said, "Ron, your decision is simple. Do what you believe God wants you to do and let God handle the consequences."

That was the beginning of one of the most meaningful relationships in my life. Dr. Stanley surprised me with his unlisted phone number and offered his continued guidance and counsel. A year and a half later, he invited me to speak at his church, and six months after that, asked me to be his special preaching assistant. For five years, I filled in when he was away and led various church outreaches. Out of that experience, I met a man who introduced me to the mentor who changed everything, Dexter Yager, who had the largest Amway business in the world.

Dexter eventually asked me to provide Christian-based motivational training for his world-wide organization. As of this writing, I have spoken live to over 8 million people in 24 countries. I have spoken at thousands of non-denominational Christian church services sponsored by hundreds of Amway business leaders (not Amway itself) and seen hundreds of thousands of people respond to a positive Christian message. All this happened because I listened both to a signal in the snow at the Shaker Village in Kentucky and the signal on the balcony at the First Baptist Church in Atlanta. I am an imperfect person with faults and limitations. I do not know why God used His signals to guide me to the opportunities I just listed. I am just humbled and grateful that He did. His divine signals led me to my purpose.

I am not saying that you need to do what I have done. You may not receive your signals the same way as me, and your purpose may be completely different. All of this may seem too mystical for you, but I believe that many of you know what I mean when I describe a sense that you are meant for something more. You recognize the restless awareness that life should be something special and that you are exceptional as well. Dr. Stanley used to urge those of us who worked with him never to choose a "settle for life." What he meant is that you can be more and do more than you ever realized. You do not have to "settle for" less than you can produce. You just need to find your purpose.

But, What If You're Wrong

But what about the possibility of making a mistake? What if you mix up your immediate desires and needs with your long-term purpose and miss your direction? What if you substitute your selfish interests for your purpose?

During my years of training with Dr. Stanley, he would often give me instruction on how to best plan my time. One afternoon he was discussing God's larger plan and reminded me that

I was still a human being with imperfect understanding. I was still capable of making mistakes. I reassured him of my determination to find and follow Gods direction, but his words had worried me. I did not want to make a mistake. I then asked Dr. Stanley what would happen if I missed Gods guidance and made the wrong decision. He laughed (kindly) and said that God was so big that my failures would not ruin his purpose. He said that God had a thousand ways to get my attention and redirect me. I just had to keep listening. Based on what he taught me, here are two comparisons that may help you understand how to handle potential miscues.

First, think of a radio or television transmitter. The signals coming from the transmitter are clear and without distortion. When they leave the equipment, they carry the right information. But their signals might be affected by interference or not received correctly because of a fault in the receiver. God is the perfect transmitter, but you are not the perfect receiver. If you think that you have made a mistake, then you should check the receiver first. Adjust the receiver (you) and try to get a more accurate reception. When you are satisfied that you have gained a better understanding of the message, then continue with your direction.

A Windy Day on a Sailboat

The second example comes from our daughter Allison. When she was in her twenties, she decided to develop her skill in several sports. She took tennis and golf lessons; then, she surprised us by adding sailing to her list. We found a lake two hours away where she could take sailing lessons. Allison worked spent hours learning how to operate these boats without motors.

Amy's parents live on the Jersey Shore, near the Shrewsbury River, a waterway that empties into the Atlantic Ocean. After Allison completed her instruction at the small lake in Kentucky, she asked if she could try her new skills on the broad river near her grandparent's home. Because the winds and currents near the ocean are so different (and dangerous) from what she had experienced on the lake, we arranged for her to take another lesson from a sailing academy in New Jersey. This proved to be a wise decision because the day she launched her tiny, two- person sailboat into the broad river basin, the wind was strong and challenging. We watched as Allison and her brother Jonathan sailed the boat away from the beach and into the current. For a few minutes, the wind remained straight, and she smoothly guided the craft into the middle of the bay. But then the wind began to swirl in different directions, and the small boat was unable to make any progress. Allison and Jonathan were stuck and could not cause the boat to turn for the return to the launch site. It was at that moment that her training told her what to do. She turned the boat into the wind and followed the wind surge until it changed, and when it changed, she changed with it. She then maneuvered the boat back and forth using the winds gusts to move the boat in the direction of the shore. In about ten minutes, the boat was secure on the beach, and Allison and Jonathan were standing safe on the sand. The different technique Allison used is "tacking." The person who pilots the boat "zigzags" back and forth using the changing wind bursts to move the vehicle in the desired direction. This is what you can do in your life when you think you are moving in a mistaken direction. You can change the flow and keep changing until you find the correct route. You do not stay "stuck." If you realize that you have made a wrong decision, then you "tack" until you find the right direction. This is 'the scientific method." In the scientific method, you test what you think is correct, and if the test proves wrong, then you test a new idea. If you think you have made a mistake, simply change to a new approach and keep moving forward. You do not need to live in fear of mistakes. As Dr. Stanley said, when you are trying to listen to God, He has a thousand ways to show you what to do.

Peace and Calm

An important indicator that you are traveling in the right direction is the sense of peace and calm that can assure you that you on the right path. Often, a sense of concern and uneasiness can be a warning, and a sense of right and calm can be a sign of the right choice.

The Wife's Warning

Amy and I have friends who recently investigated a business opportunity. The offer was to partner in the development of a chain of fitness centers. The husband was convinced that the opportunity was an excellent chance to create a profit, but the wife was not. The couple asked to speak with us, and we arranged a meeting. The husband excitedly described the potential of the business. He assured us that he had studied the business plan carefully and believed that the business would be a great success. He saw little risk. I asked about his financial investment, and he said that he would need to place a substantial amount into the business to complete the deal. He was ready to empty his (and his wife's) savings to create the partnership.

During the conversation, his wife projected nervousness and uncertainty. When I asked what she thought, she said that she considered the project a mistake. Her husband interrupted and reminded her that they had already discussed the details and that he had explained how the arrangement worked. The wife looked up and said that she had no objection to the business plan. Her problem was the partnership agreement. She said that when she met the man who would be the other partner, she had an immediate sense of distrust. She agreed that the man was charming and open but could not shake a sense of unease.

The husband was very respectful to his wife but insisted that the other man was a reputable and capable businessman and could be trusted. The wife was equally respectful of her husband but said she did not agree. We had known this couple for several years and knew they had a healthy and loving marriage. Even during our conversation, they were polite and careful of one another's feelings. But, even with this solid foundation, they could not agree on the partnership. He remained convinced that was "a good deal," and she continued to have no sense of peace and confirmation. The husband invested the money and enacted the partnership. The venture eventually failed because the partner proved to be dishonest and deceitful. The couple lost several million dollars and took years to recover financially. The wife had been right. I am not saying that you should always follow your feelings. You should, of course, investigate your options and research your opportunities. You should gather facts and ask questions. You should verify what people say and confirm what people claim. But when you have done all, you can, you should then listen to the small voice within that either confirms or denies your choice. Dr. Stanley told me that, after he had checked into the details of a decision, he still waited for a sense of peace to move forward. He said that he had learned never to proceed without that confirming sense of peace and rightness.

I encourage you to do two things. You should "do your homework" and prepare for your decisions, AND you should arrive at a sense of peace before you go forward. In my experience, I have always regretted it when I ignored a feeling that something was wrong or "off" but proceeded anyway. I also encourage you to avoid being paralyzed by the fear of wrong decisions. You will make mistakes. That is an unavoidable part of being a human being. But you can learn from your mistakes and "tack" with the changing winds to recover your direction.

The Hiker

I am a passionate and avid hiker. I have followed trails in the Rocky Mountains of the United States and Canada, the great Southern Appalachians, the National Parks of Yellowstone, and Yosemite, the European Alps, the Blue Mountains of Australia, and the rolling hills of the Lake District in England and one thing has always been constant. You guide yourself with a focus on a fixed point, whether a specific star in the night sky or a particular peak on a mountain. You may meander and curve and temporarily lose sight of your guiding point, but you always refocus on its location and follow it to your goal. That is what it means to be guided by your purpose.

The Dangerous Bridge

Several years ago, I was invited to speak in Northern Ireland. I had always wanted to visit Ireland because my Mother's family had immigrated to the United States from Belfast in the nineteenth century. I arranged to take Amy and Allison with me, and we arrived in Belfast full of anticipation and excitement. We were escorted to a charming inn that matched everything we had imagined Ireland to be. The first morning we enjoyed a traditional Irish breakfast (I loved it!) and prepared for the convention. I spoke throughout the weekend. The event was an excellent success, and we finished, thankful, and tired.

The next day the owner of the company that sponsored the convention arranged a unique excursion for our family. After another substantial Irish breakfast, we were driven by our host up the northeastern Irish coastline. It was a brisk early June morning with light snow mixed with intermittent sunshine. We were surprised by snow in June, and our guide explained that our location near the Arctic Circle brought occasional bursts of wintry weather in the Spring. The highway we traveled eventually turned into a small one-lane road. We frequently stopped to allow small flocks of sheep to cross the road and finally arrived at our destination, the Giants Causeway. The Giant's Causeway is one of the most unusual and dramatic geological sites in the world. It is a formation of 40,000 interlocking basalt columns on the northern Irish coast on the edge of the Irish Sea. The columns have nearly perfect smooth sides and spread along this section of the coast and onto the edge of the violent surf.

We parked the car and explored the area for almost an hour. The sky had cleared, and a brilliant blue sky covered us. Tie sunshine warmed the air, which was so clear that we could see the coast of Scotland in the distance. When we finished our examination of the area, I noticed a small island about 50 yards beyond the edge of the causeway, connected to the mainland by a rope bridge floored by narrow wooden slats. I decided to walk the bridge to the island and asked if anyone wanted to come with me. Amy and our host said no, but our curious and brave daughter said yes. Allison's mom intervened and said it was too dangerous for a child and expressed doubts about the idea for adults as well. I agreed to cross alone and walked to the edge of the bridge. The wind had increased, and the bridge swayed back and forth. When I stepped onto the bridge, I looked down and saw that the wooden slats were each separated by two inches, and I could see through them to the wild waves crashing against the rocks a hundred feet below. The currents swirled savagely, and the spray was tossed so high in the air that I felt the mist on my face.

As I stepped on to bridge, I felt the wind carry me from side to side as I rocked back and forth. I stopped and held onto the rope sides and wondered if I could continue. I was scared, and every time I looked down, my fear increased. I then looked across to the Island and saw a giant boulder in the middle of the property. I decided to use the stone to guide me across. I fixed my eyes on the rock and kept my focus on the boulder as I moved my feet. Step by step, I continued crossing the bridge, never taking my gaze from the stone until I stepped onto the island with an enormous sense of relief. I felt a surge of accomplishment. I had reached my goal! It only took a few minutes to explore the small island, but the spectacular view was worth the effort. The Scottish coast was even closer, and the Irish Sea spread, blue and vivid before me. It was exhilarating.

When the excitement faded, I realized that to return, I would need to cross the dangerous bridge again. I walked to the edge and saw Allison on the causeway. I waved and motioned for her to remain on her spot. I then focused on my daughter as I had focused on the boulder and used that focus to guide me across the bridge. The bridge still swayed, and the waves continued to crash, but my concentration on Allison brought me back to safety. Amy, Allison, and our host helped me celebrate my achievement; then we returned to the car for the drive back to the Inn. It was a memorable experience.

When you encounter difficulties and disappointments in the pursuit of your purpose, remember this lesson. When you focus on your objective, you gain energy and determination. Your fear will fade when you concentrate on where you want to go. When I made reaching the boulder my goal, that fixation helped me move through the obstacles and dangers to arrive at my destination. When I made Allison my goal on the return, she guided me back, although my environment was just as dangerous as before. In both cases, focusing on the goal kept me on track. When you keep your focus on your goal, you can plow through challenges because the goal is connected to your purpose. You can use a star in the night sky, the peak of a mountain, or a boulder and a little girl on each side of a dangerous bridge to direct your steps. In the same way, your goals guide and empower you.

I believe that your vital purpose is rooted in your place in God's creation. That means that you have a mission to fulfill and a purpose to complete. The first two chapters of this book are to help you find your purpose. Life is empty without a purpose, and I believe that one of the significant challenges of our time is that many people think that their purpose is themselves. I support and encourage personal development and self-improvement, but even personal growth is meaningless without a reason for the development.

The Reason I Flew First Class

I was speaking at a convention in Atlanta. I finished my final session at noon and departed for the airport so I could get a flight to my next speaking engagement in Los Angeles. The meeting went longer than expected, and when I concluded my speech, I went directly to a waiting car and hurried to the airport. The Atlanta-Hartsfield Airport is one of the busiest in the world, and as I fought my way through the crowds, I prayed I would reach my flight in time. I rode a jammed underground train to a distant concourse, exited, and ran toward the gate, rolling my carry-on bag behind me. I arrived at the entrance and saw no one in line with a lone gate agent standing at the door. I approached her and prepared to argue to be allowed onto the plane. But the agent surprised me when she asked if I was Mr. Ball. When I said yes, she handed me a boarding pass and said that a special arrangement had been made for me. She then stepped aside so I could enter the aircraft. As I entered, I glanced at the boarding pass and saw that I was seated in first class, although I had not bought a first- class ticket. I rarely traveled first class because of the expense. I found my seat, stored my bag, and settled in. A flight attendant brought me water and a menu so I could select one of several meals offered. I chose my food and returned the list.

I was impressed by the quiet and extended space of the first-class compartment and began to enjoy the special attention given to me by the attendant. Then something else happened. I started to feel a sense of superiority to the passengers in the coach-economy section. Although I had bought a ticket that made me one of them, I thought that I must be deserving of better treatment. I began to see myself as an elite and not like the other passengers who were prohibited from my first-class cabin. Then, just as quickly, something else happened. I heard an inner voice telling me that I had done nothing to deserve my upgrade and was no better than the passengers in the cheaper section. My inner voice said to me that God had blessed me with my unexpected (and unpurchased) seat so I could rest and be in better condition for the responsibilities waiting for me when I landed. My upgrade was not to exalt me and inflate my ego; it was to help me better serve other people. It was to help me fulfill my purpose. I asked for forgiveness for my selfish response and felt a rush of humility and gratitude. I had received a gift so that I could be a gift to someone else.

I include this story to explain that when you receive blessings and support, it is not just about you. When you improve yourself, it is so you can better fulfill your purpose. When you focus on personal development as your primary goal, you mistakenly make the means the end. Your progress should have a purpose. Your improvement should enable you to accomplish something more important.

The Young Bodybuilder

I spoke with a young woman following one of my seminars who was in her early twenties. The purpose of the seminar was to introduce attendees to techniques that would help them read body language and better understand how to interact with people effectively. The young woman was developing a new business concept and had come to the seminar to improve her "people skills." She was bright, enthusiastic, and likable. She had a degree in marketing from a prestigious university and was ready to advance. As we talked, ideas and goals spilled from her mouth, and her excitement was contagious. She then added that she was equally committed to her physical development. She went to a gym early each morning to lift weights and do aerobic exercise. She so liked the weight training that she had signed up for a bodybuilding program and planned to enter a competition. When she paused, I asked her a question. I asked her why she was building her business. She answered that she wanted to "be successful." I asked her why she wanted to be successful, and she said she wanted a "better life." I then asked her why she was so devoted to physical fitness, and she said that she wanted to look good and be healthy. I asked her why she wanted to look good and be healthy. She said that she wanted those results because they "were good things" At this point, I realized that this attractive, energetic, focused young woman was pursuing herself, not her purpose. Everything she listed as a reason for her decisions was an action that led back to herself. It was as if her life was a giant circle, with everything eventually leading back to herself. There was no purpose beyond her self-improvement. That is the reason she could not explain "why" she was doing what she was doing; she could only continue to "do" what she was doing.

This young woman is representative of millions of well- intentioned individuals who see life as endless self-advancement. Many of them believe that the most crucial goal in life is to "be yourself" or to "find yourself." They have grown up believing that their "self-esteem" is fundamental to happiness. They are people who believe that the goal in life is "to be the best you can be," but do not know WHY you should be your best. This approach breeds shallow and disappointed people who wake up one day and wonder what their life means. They have missed their mission.

As I said earlier, I believe in the value of personal development. I endorse physical fitness and intellectual improvement. I encourage you to learn new skills and discover new knowledge. But I also believe that you are here for a reason and your development is to help you "be the best you can be" because of that reason. I have asked many people to tell me what motivates them for success and achievement. Some speak of possessions they hope to own and experiences they want to have, but many go more in-depth and tell me that they work hard so they can help their aging parents or increase opportunities for their children. Others say they dream of helping the sick or want to alleviate suffering. Some are inspired to build and grow because they see all around them various human needs that are unmet and are not satisfied until someone does something to meet those needs. I have heard from Individuals who make money to build churches and raise hospitals. These are people who cannot rest until they do something good. *These* people understand their purpose. It is not all about them.

CHAPTER 4
What's in Your Box?

You need to be sure of two things if you want to discover and fulfill your purpose. You need to know what your purpose is, and you need to know how to make it happen. Over the first two chapters, I have written about the need to find your purpose and to understand and accurately interpret the signals that come to guide you. But I want to help you make sure that you know where to find your purpose. It may be hidden right in front of you.

I encountered a man many years ago who taught me this vital lesson. He was a successful movie and television producer who had a friend who owned several television stations in Texas. His friend had developed his business "from the ground up" and was a multi-millionaire in his mid-forties. He was married with one son. His friend's world crashed around him when his young adult son was killed in an accident. The man and his wife were numb with grief and unable to function. Their money and success suddenly seemed meaningless. The man contacted his friend in Hollywood and asked for prayer and help. The Texas couple were devout Christians and knew their producer friend shared their faith. The producer answered with a pledge of prayer and then offered some advice. He told the man that he knew someone in New York who could help the couple in their time of suffering. His friend agreed that he and his wife needed help and asked for more information. The producer offered to arrange a meeting but told the man that the individual in New York would not be what they expected. He explained that the man in New York was a highly respected consultant who only worked with elite clients. There was no guarantee he would agree to meet the couple. In addition, there was one more thing; the consultant was a Jewish atheist who certainly did not have the same worldview as the Christian couple. But, the producer added, he believed that the consultant could give the couple the guidance they needed.

The consultant agreed to help, and a meeting was arranged in Florida. The couple flew to the location, and the meeting began. The consultant was polite and offered his condolences on the death of their son. The couple responded with appreciation and invited the consultant to give his input. The couple admitted that they no longer had a reason to live and hoped the consultant could offer something that could lift them from their depression. The consultant said that he wanted, first, to tell them a story. He then said to them that he had been hired a few years before by the Coca-Cola corporation to help them at times of crisis. The company had changed the formula for its soft drink to make it sweeter. They chose to sweeten the product to better compete with Pepsi, their nearest rival. They named the replacement beverage, "New Coke." New Coke was a disaster. Customers hated it. The change in formula caused a customer revolt. The company was losing enormous amounts of money and faced even more losses in the future. The Board of Directors scheduled an emergency session and asked the New York consultant to join them. The consultant told the couple from Texas that after meeting with the Board, he decided on a radical strategy. He left the room and returned a few minutes later with an ordinary cardboard box. He placed the box on the table and told each Board member to write on a piece of paper what he or she considered to be the primary purpose of the Coca-Cola company. He told the Board members that he would come back to the room in fifteen minutes. He instructed them to place their notes in the box when they finished. When he reentered the room, everyone was quiet. No one spoke or moved as he picked up the box. The consultant opened the box and read each entry. To everyone's surprise, most of the notes had the same idea, in various forms. Most read that the purpose of the company was to "preserve and continue the tradition of a great American product." After the consultant had read aloud each comment, he said that the mission of the company was clear, to do what was "in the box."

The Coca-Cola company immediately reintroduced classic coke and removed New Coke from the shelves. The change reinvigorated the company and reenergized the brand. The tradition of a great American product had been saved. The consultant finished his story and excused himself.

After a few minutes, he returned and placed a simple cardboard box on a table in front of the couple. He handed them two index cards and two pens and told them to write what they believed to be the purpose they were supposed to pursue for the rest of their lives. They should be careful and ONLY place in the box what they believed to be their mission. He told them to take as much time as they needed and to knock on the door when they finished.

The couple was confused and angry. They had come for counsel and were disappointed by the consultant's request. But after several minutes, they calmed and realized the value of doing what he asked. They talked, prayed, and thought. Eventually, they felt ready to complete their assignment. They each wrote their conclusion on the card and placed it in the box. Then the husband rose from his seat and knocked on the door. When the consultant returned, he opened the box and lifted out the two cards. On each was written the same purpose statement. The husband and wife both believed that their new mission was to fund and develop schools in underdeveloped countries and underserved areas of the United States in honor and memory of their son. Their child had not had the opportunity to fulfill his life so they would help give an opportunity to other young men and women to fulfill their lives. The consultant told the couple that they had identified their mission. The couple thanked the consultant, flew home, and for the remainder of their lives, followed their purpose. Their joy returned, and the surge of their new purpose carried them forward.

Do you want to find your mission and realize your purpose? Then you need to answer one question.

What's in Your Box?

What is the one thing that will give your life meaning and value? Open your box and find out.

CHAPTER 5
The Goal Ladder

You need to climb up a series of steps to fulfill your purpose. These steps are called goals. The "goal ladder" is made of steps that lead you in the right direction. A goal, of course, can be a limited objective without deep meaning. You can have a "goal" to cut your grass by Thursday or to complete a project at work. If you own your own business, you may have a specific sales goal or a goal to hire someone to help you. But there is a different type of goal that is much more important. These goals are the rungs on the ladder that lift you up to the level of your purpose. These are the goals that are part of the process that carries you forward.

The Confused Couple

I met a dynamic Hispanic couple while I was speaking at a marketing convention in the northwestern United States. I was impressed with their intelligence and commitment to success. They were goal-driven and had already developed a profitable business. They understood the necessity of hard work and were willing to sacrifice to achieve their dreams. Amy and I went to lunch with this couple during a break in the convention program and enjoyed their excitement and vision. While at lunch, I asked the couple about their goal. The wife answereci with a list of "goals" that related to their business. They hoped to expand the business and had formulated a plan to make that happen. I listened and then asked my question again. They seemed confused and repeated their list. I then politely explained that I was asking about their "goal," not their "goals." I wanted to know WHY they were building their business. What they had done was to give me information about specific parts of their business process. What they told me was important but still not the reason for their efforts. I then told them the story of the "mysterious box." When I finished, I simply asked, "what's in your box?"

The couple looked at one another, then faced me. They became more serious and asked if they could tell me a story. The husband told me about the village he had grown up in rural Mexico. His grandmother had lived for years in a three-sided shack that was completely open on one side. The only privacy was a sheet hung over a piece of rope. The grandmother planted and harvested a small garden every year, providing food for her and her daughter. When the daughter married, she and her husband added another shack to the property and enlarged the garden. They had three children, two daughters, and a boy. That boy was the husband telling me the story.

At this point, the husband began to cry. He said that he and his wife were expanding their business to enable them to bring their family to the United States. His wife had been born in Sacramento, California, and her parents were United States citizens. He told me that his wife loved his family and was equally committed to helping his mother, father, and grandmother find a new life. When the husband finished, he said, "that is what is in our box." I thanked the couple for sharing their story and assured them of my respect for their commitment to helping his family. I told them that what they had communicated with me was their final GOAL, which was not the same as the smaller goals required to reach the big goal.

This is the meaning of the "goal ladder." The goals the couple described to expand their business were the rungs of the ladder they needed to climb to arrive at the final "purpose-goal" at the top. The goal at the top was their true purpose. I spoke with this couple a year and a half later. They told me that their business was booming, and they had been able to bring the husband's family to the United States. I congratulated them then asked what their mission was now. The wife smiled and said that as their business and expanded, so had their purpose. They were now helping other Hispanic men and women develop successful businesses so they could be in a financial position to help and bless their families as well. Their true "big" goal was still alive. There is an essential difference between the minor goals of ordinary life and the goals that help you fulfill your purpose. But how do you know the difference?

A Fourteen-Year-Old Discovers His Purpose

The first United States President, George Washington, composed a remarkable book as a young man. When Washington was fourteen years old, he made a list of 110 *Rules of Civility.* The "rules" were based on behavioral guidelines that had been circulating in France since the sixteenth century. Young Washington recorded the rules in a schoolbook and studied them regularly. Many historians believe they are an insight into the character of the first American president.

Washington was known in his time as a man characterized by commitment to duty. He was trusted by his fellow citizens because of his reputation for fearless integrity and personal sacrifice. He was famous for what educated people in the eighteenth century called "disinterest." In our modern understanding, this is a selfless commitment to actions that benefit other people. Disinterest simply means a "disinterest" in yourself when you make decisions that affect other people. This why Washington was later called "the indispensable man" by historian James Thomas Flexner. He was "indispensable" because he was the one leader everyone trusted.

Washington, as a young man, made a commitment to duty his guiding principle, and this led him to his mission to save and govern the new Republic. But the 110 maxims of conduct he listed at fourteen were his "mission goals." They were steps on his ladder that lifted him to his life purpose. A careful look at Washington's *Rules of Civility* reveals many principles that encourage a person to deal with others with respect. According to the "Rules," everything a person does should be guided by a duty to care for other people. These "Rules" formed the basis of Washingtons character and made him the "indispensable man" whose purpose was to fulfill his duty to help other people.

His rule number 48 says, "Wherein you reprove another be unblameable yourself; for example, is more prevalent [important] than precepts [words]".

Washington used reminders like this to give him the strength to do his duty as an adult. They were steps on his ladder of success. They taught him courtesy and respect toward other people and made men want to follow him. Parson Weems, Washington's first biographer wrote that it was "no wonder everybody honored him who honored everybody." The *Rules of Civility* that Washington followed his entire life were the "rungs" (goals) of the ladder he climbed to reach the "big "goal of his purpose.

The Chocolate Souffle

Amy was in the final weeks of her pregnancy with our first child (our daughter Allison). I decided to surprise her with a night out. I secretly packed a suitcase and placed it in our car, then asked her to come with me to a "meeting." We drove to a downtown hotel in Atlanta, where I had reserved a table at a restaurant (I had also reserved a room for the night, unknown to Amy). We parked, entered the hotel, and went to the restaurant. When Amy asked where the meeting was, I told her the meeting was with her. She laughed and thanked me for arranging a special evening.

We enjoyed the excellent food for which the restaurant was known and decided to add dessert. I asked our server for a recommendation, and she said that the best dessert offered was a chocolate souffle. We had never had this dessert and quickly ordered one. The server said that each soufflé was individually prepared and asked if it would be alright if we waited 30 minutes for its arrival. We said yes and settled into our wait. While we waited, I asked Amy if there was anything she wanted to discuss about the new baby and our immediate future. She said that she had just listened to an audio about goal setting and asked if we could make a list of our goals while we sat. I agreed, and Amy produced a pen and paper from her purse. What began to fill the time became an exercise that altered the direction of our lives. We had never written down our goals. We had discussed what we hoped for but had never made a specific list. That night, waiting for the soufflé, we shared with honesty and enthusiasm what we each wanted to happen.

We focused, at first, on the baby and our plans for our expanding family but soon shifted to what we believed God wanted us to accomplish. We started with a discussion of houses, nurseries, and future schools and moved to an examination of what our life together should mean. It was the first time we had arrived at a clear and specific understanding of our mutual purpose. We realized that we shared a calling to help people by giving them Gods principles. We wanted to introduce men and women to the Savior, who had transformed us.

Then something else happened. As we recorded our goals and desires, we realized that to fulfill our purpose, we needed goals that would take us, step by step, where we wanted to go. We ended with two lists. Our personal "quality of life" goals such as a bigger house in a better neighborhood or newer, safer car were on one list, and our life goals were on another list. Both lists were legitimate, we just needed to balance them, so the first one would not interfere with the second. What we learned during our unexpected exercise was that it is alright to have both personal goals (that make you happy and improve your life) and life-purpose goals that drive and satisfy your life, if they do not contradict each other.

It is not wrong to work for a car, a house, or a family vacation, but those "things"[5] should never be a substitute for your life purpose. When possessions or experiences replace your purpose, your life becomes empty and sterile. That is the root of the restlessness that reminds you of what you are missing. But when you make your life purpose your priority, then these other things can be rewards along the way that you can enjoy without guilt. A purpose-driven life can still be filled with fun experiences and new possessions if they do not "take over" and replace your purpose.

One definition of materialism is "the worship of the material, the belief that your true meaning in life is the material object you want to possess." But no experience or possession can provide meaning and purpose. Those things and experiences are just enjoyable additions to the journey. I love sweets, but if I tried to live on milkshakes, cakes, and candy, I would not receive the nourishment required for a long and healthy life. The same is true of material possessions and personal experiences. They are momentary rewards. They are not a substitute for your purpose. During our time at the Atlanta restaurant, we saw the motivational power of both sets of goals and learned to blend the personal and the purposeful. And, when the souffle came, it was terrific.

The Goal Parade

When you list your goals, they are like a parade surging forward. A parade moves in a positive direction and is filled with both purpose and excitement. It has both direction and celebration. It offers fun and meaning. Think of your goals as a parade moving through your life. The parade is filled with fun but should still have a meaningful destination. Parades should still have a purpose. As you march with the parade, you should make certain that your goals have specific characteristics. Your regular goals should always help you fulfill the goal of your life purpose. The following is a list that explains how your "ordinary" goals can contribute to the "big" goal of your life purpose.

Strategic Goals

great importance within an integrated whole..." It means that your goals should fit your life-plan and help you accomplish your purpose.

The Couple with Different Goals

I once worked with a couple who were in their fifties with a successful business. They had just sold their house and were debating where to live. They had consulted me on some spiritual matters and asked if I could help them analyze their choices. I asked the husband if he had a location he preferred, and he mentioned a town in Florida where he and his wife had vacationed. He said it had everything he wanted, boating, fishing, and charming local restaurants.

As he spoke, I noticed that his wife seemed uneasy, so when he finished, I asked her where she wanted to live. She said that their three children and two grandchildren lived in the largest city of their state, and she had hoped to relocate near them.

The husband turned to his wife and said he thought that she wanted to enjoy the climate and recreational opportunities of Florida. She agreed that Florida offered exceptional weather and outside activities but insisted that she preferred to near her family.

I asked what they wanted most in this chapter of their lives, and they again gave different answers. I suggested that they spend some time politely discussing why they wanted each option and then return to examine their conclusions. They left so they could speak in private.

Four hours later, the couple returned, and it was apparent that something had changed. The husband explained that when he imagined their ongoing life, he realized that he wanted the same thing as his wife. He wanted to be with his children and watch his grandchildren grow up. He decided that Florida vacations would always be available, but his family might not. His wife was joyous at the prospect of reuniting her clan, and the two had already begun to plan where to live. They could now make a strategic goal that fit their long-term purpose. They moved, and everyone was happy and satisfied.

When I last checked, the couple (and their children, married spouses, and grandchildren) were all happy and satisfied. The couple made a "strategic" decision based on a "strategic" goal.

The Wrong Boat

Decisions are simpler when they are part of a larger plan that includes your purpose. I once spoke with a friend who wanted to buy a (big) boat he could not easily afford. His brother had a similar boat and consistently spoke of the fun it brought his family. My friend became obsessed with the boat and talked about it constantly. When he asked me what I thought, I asked him about his long-term purpose and if the boat fit that purpose (a strategic goal). He admitted that he was in financial difficulty, and his business was in a slump. His dream was to build his business to a level where it could sustain him while he and his wife supported mission trips from his church. When I said that the boat did not seem to fit his long-term purpose, he agreed that it would not advance his lifegoals. In other words, it was not a "strategic goal" because it did not fit his on-going purpose.

This does not mean that owning a boat is a bad thing. It means that the boat was not a strategic goal that would move him forward. He decided not to buy the boat. He even realized that he wanted the boat for the wrong reason, to compete with his brother rather than to bless his family. Five years later, when his business had tripled, and he had no debt, he retired, became the mission director at his church, for no salary....and bought a boat.

Sustainable Goals

The Mysterious House

An intermediary goal should add sustainability to the pursuit of your lifegoal. During my time as the special preaching assistant to Dr. Charles Stanley at the First Baptist Church in Atlanta, a man in the church approached me and asked if he could show me a property. He had discovered a particular house and grounds on the edge of an upscale area of the city and thought it had extraordinary potential. It was hidden from the main road behind enormous magnolia trees and reached by a long winding driveway. He asked if I would like to see it. I was not looking for property but was curious and said yes.

He drove me through expensive neighborhoods dominated by perfect lawns and over-sized houses. We arrived at the property and entered the driveway. We followed a curve and stopped in front of the house. It had been a remarkable mansion at one time, but looked dilapidated, surrounded by out-of-control shrubbery and waist-high weeds. We parked and went in through a side door. The house was brilliantly designed. It had enormous windows looking out on what, at one time, were expansive, cultivated lawns. The rooms were large, with expensive, custom-made features. I was especially interested in the master bedroom, which opened onto an Italian style patio centered by an elaborate fountain. The doors and windows facing the outside were all glass and spread from wall to wall and from ceiling to floor. An electronically controlled shade was positioned to darken the room to create a sleeping environment. With some repair and cleaning, it could be a spectacular property.

When I left the house, I was convinced that Amy and I had to buy it. I did not know the price and did not care. On the drive home, I asked my friend to research the price and current ownership so I could make a purchase offer. A few days later, he contacted me with the owner's information and the price. To my disappointment, it was far beyond my financial ability. Even if I could quickly sell our modest home, I would not be even close to the amount required. I took Amy to see the property and, although she agreed it was a fantastic home, she thought we could not afford it. For the next two weeks, I became obsessed with the house and tried to calculate different ways to make the purchase. We were in a significant expansion at the church, and I was responsible for part of the project, but I was continually distracted by thoughts of the property.

I finally decided to discuss my options with Dr. Stanley. I described the house in detail, praised its location, and painted a picture of what, I believed, it could become. Dr. Stanley listened carefully, then asked me a series of questions that brought me back to reality. He first asked about our financial resources (not enough), then asked how much money I estimated for the renovations (a lot), then asked how the house fit my goals for our future. I answered his questions then told him that the owner of the house had just offered to finance the home if I would sign a commitment to add a large sum of money to the payments every few months. These payments would be in addition to a base payment I already could not afford. Each added amount was more than I made in a year.

Dr. Stanley looked surprised then told me that not only was it a wrong financial decision, but even if I could make the payments for a few months, the situation was not sustainable. There was no logical way I could keep such a plan going. Everything would eventually collapse. Dr. Stanley prayed with me, reminded me that it was my decision, not his, and I left.

I struggled for two days. A battle raged between my heart and my head, between my desires and wisdom. But one thing Dr. Stanley said finally made my decision. He was right. My goal was not SUSTAINABLE. It would undermine my ability to fulfill my true purpose. I declined the offer.

Instantly a sense of calm filled my heart. I knew I had made the right choice. You may pick a goal, in a surge of excitement, but you still need to determine if your goal is sustainable. If not, then the goal will become a burden that weighs you down and drains your energy. It will sap your strength and steal your peace. You should always measure your resources and determine if you have the inner and outer ingredients to make the plan work. You should do nothing to block your purpose.

Stunning Goals

Your major life goals should be so stunning that they stretch you to achieve more. This may seem contradictory to the previous point, but it is not for one reason. A goal can inspire you to great action and still be sustainable. The non-sustainable goal is not supported by your abilities or commitment. You just cannot keep going. But the stunning goal excites and motivates you because it elevates you. The stunning goal is worth the effort. The unsustainable goal is simply a bad decision. When you commit to a goal, make certain that the goal is an exciting, "stunning" addition that empowers you toward your life-purpose.

The Football Dream

I have shared a speaking platform several times with a remarkable individual. He is friendly and out-going, and I have always liked him. I like his story even better.

I first met Daniel Ruettiger at a motivational conference, where we were both scheduled to speak. We spent almost an hour backstage, and I appreciated that he was uninflated by his fame and was considerate and polite to everyone he encountered. When he was introduced to the pumped-up crowd of 36,000 people, he smiled and waved to the excited audience. The giant screen behind him blazed to life, and everyone watched a scene from the movie based on his accomplishments. When the clip ended, the arena erupted with an explosion of sound, and the crowd began chanting his nickname, "Rudy, Rudy, Rudy."

Daniel "Rudy" Ruettiger had a stunning life goal. He was only five feet six inches tall and weighed 165 pounds, but he dreamed of playing football for the University of Notre Dame, the pinnacle of success for a Catholic boy like Rudy.

Rudy was one of fourteen children, who was born and grew up in Joliet, Illinois. He played football at Joliet Catholic High School but struggled in class. He finished high school and joined the United States Navy. After two years in the Navy, he worked in a power plant for two additional years. During this time, his stunning dream continued to smolder in his heart. He applied to Notre Dame but was rejected because of his poor high school grades and then enrolled in Holy Cross College. He continued to apply to Notre Dame until he was finally accepted on the fourth try.

Rudy worked with furious dedication and was selected for the scout team, a group of non-scholarship players who helped the main varsity team practice for games.

Then at Notre Dame's last home game of the season against Georgia Tech, in a moment made for the movies, the head coach, Dan Devine, decided to put Rudy in the game. Rudy was a senior, and this was his last chance to participate in an actual game. He made the most of his opportunity. He was in the game for three plays and recorded a sack of the Georgia Tech quarterback on the final play of the game. His ecstatic teammates carried him off the field in celebration of the win and Rudy's improbable accomplishment. He was the first player in the 87-year (to that point) history of Notre Dame football to receive that honor.

In 1993, the film *Rudy* was released in theaters and continues to inspire people to pursue their dreams. If Rudy had not had a stunning goal, none of this would have happened.

I shared the stage with Rudy several times over several years, and he was always the same friendly, warm-hearted man who was polite to everyone. He was also the man whose stunning goal has motivated millions. I am not saying that the only worthy goals are ones that have movies made about them. I am telling you should aim for goals that have the power to stun you into action. They should increase your commitment and energize your life. They should cause you to give "furious dedication." They should inspire you to greatness. They should accelerate you toward your purpose.

Simple Goals

A goal does not need to be complicated to lead to greatness. The simpler the goal, the easier it is to organize and execute your plan toward your purpose.

The Front Porch

When I was fifteen, my parents bought their first home. It was a small house in our small town in eastern Kentucky on a street that followed a winding river. The house has a front porch that faces a tree-covered mountain on the far side of the river. I was studying the Bible intensively and searching for ways to experience closeness with God during the year we moved. I was a new Christian and eager to grow in my spiritual relationship.

After the move, I spent time each week sitting on the front porch, praying, and thinking. I had recently discovered the ministry of Billy Graham and developed a desire to communicate my experience with Jesus Christ to large numbers of people.

One Saturday afternoon, I was on the porch reading a history of Christian outreach when I found a story about the nineteenth- century evangelist D. L. Moody. The book said that Moody was "the Billy Graham" of the nineteenth century and famous for speaking to crowds of thousands of people in what he called "campaigns." The story was an account of visits to Oxford and Cambridge Universities in England by Moody during one of his national "campaigns." Moody encountered open hostility in both institutions, but his honest and straightforward messages won over the students and faculty of both schools.

The highlight of his visit to Oxford was a public assembly attended by several thousand people where Moody spoke. The meeting opened with jeers and insults directed toward Moody and his team, but Moody's loving sincerity and clear, convincing words captured the audience. When Moody asked for a public expression from those who wanted to make a commitment to Christ, hundreds responded. Moody wept with emotion and, turning to an associate, said, "My God, this is worth living for!"

When I finished the story, I was as moved as Moody. I looked over at the side of the mountain and imagined the thousands of trees as thousands of people. I felt a calling to speak publicly to mass meetings where people could hear the positive, life-affirming message of Jesus Christ. I had no speaking experience and lived in an isolated, remote section of the Cumberland Mountains but knew that I wanted to learn to communicate to as many people as possible.

The lifegoal that was born at that moment on the front porch was stunning (to me), and it was also simple. It was a clear definition of what I felt called to do. I have pursued one goal for decades. This simple goal of learning to speak to large groups of people fit my mission of explaining Gods principles of a happy and successful life to as many people as possible. A simple goal that helps you fulfill your purpose is a goal you can believe in.

The Worldwide Business

My friend and mentor, Dexter Yager, who built the largest Amway business in the world at that time, told me that he was in his late twenties when he discovered the Amway opportunity. He said that he had sold cars and driven a delivery truck but was looking for a vehicle to help him accomplish his mission.

Dexter said that his purpose was to create financial independence for himself, his family, and other people so that everyone could have the freedom to pursue Gods purpose without restraint or restriction. When he was introduced to Amway, he said that he realized that it was a SIMPLE way to accomplish his purpose. All he had to do was to follow the business model for himself and introduce it to other people. He stayed focused on this simple model for the rest of his life and used it to fulfill his greater purpose.

Dexter's Amway organization now stretches around the world. Millions of people have been helped and influenced by his leadership. His simple commitment to a simple approach kept him and his mission on track. Try to isolate the simple, core goals and actions that will enhance your success. Do not allow yourself to be detoured away from your main mission.

Specific Goals

The list of goals that Amy and I made at the downtown Atlanta hotel was the first specific list we had ever composed. We had always had goals, but they were general and vague. We wanted to be happy, we wanted to pay our bills, and we wanted to serve God. All these were good objectives, but none were specific and clear. Our list that evening was different. It contained exactly what we wanted to do and precisely where we wanted to go. That list changed our direction and empowered our lives.

The Woman Who Wanted Money

I was speaking at a financial seminar in Chicago. Hundreds of excited people were jammed into the hotel ballroom with dozens standing in the hallway, listening through the open doors. I sensed an atmosphere of anticipation. People seemed eager to start.

I began with a story about a man who had created financial freedom for his family. I gave details about his approach and why it worked. I emphasized his commitment to specific financial goals. I then asked everyone to write in their notebooks, one specific financial goal. The audience grew quiet as the participants engaged in the exercise. When the time allotted for the exercise expired, I asked everyone to put down their notebooks and look at me. Next, I asked for volunteers to share what they had written. Two men stood and read their input. Then a woman in the back stood and asked if she could say something before, she shared her goal. I agreed, and she began. She said that her goal was simple and specific. She wanted more money. She was positive and outgoing, so I thought she would not mind being part of an experiment. I thanked her and asked if she would walk to the front of the stage. When she arrived, I withdrew my wallet and took out a one-dollar bill. I handed her the currency and said, "congratulations, you have met your goal. You don't need to stay for the rest of the seminar. You are finished."

She seemed puzzled. She looked at the dollar bill and said that her goal was to have more money, and this was not enough. I answered that her stated goal was to have MORE money. I asked her if the addition of the dollar meant that she now had more money than she had come with, and she said yes. I then said that her goal was met because all she had asked for was more money. She laughed and said she understood the point. She thought she had expressed a specific and desirable goal but instead had

shared a vague goal that did not represent what she really wanted. When she returned to her seat, I explained that seeking "more money" or "more happiness" or "a better relationship" sound like goals but are so generalized that you could never know if you "hit the target."
Instead of seeking more money, it would be more effective, for example, to seek an after taxes income of $100,000 per year by two years from today's date. Instead of hoping for happiness, it would be better to select two organizations that you believe in and volunteer to help because when you help someone else, you often find your own happiness. Instead of wanting to lose weight, you could decide to lose one pound per month for twelve months. Based on these examples, I told everyone to take a few minutes and reexamine their goal statements and make sure they were specific. Reexamine your life goals and make sure they are exactly and specifically what you want.

Significant Goals

Here is the core difference between an "ordinary" goal and a "life goal". An ordinary goal is something that improves or advances your quality of life. It matters because it makes your life easier and solves practical problems that can interrupt the flow of your life. But a SIGNIFICANT life goal is connected to your purpose and helps empower that purpose.

How We Rediscovered Our Goals

During the coronavirus crisis, I, along with millions of others, stayed home for several weeks. I quickly recognized that the enforced separation from my usual travel and speaking schedule was an opportunity to advance both ordinary and significant goals. I, along with Amy, made a new plan. We started with a list of "ordinary" goals. We trimmed our shrubbery and mulched our yard. We emptied junk from our basement that we had wanted to eliminate for several years. We painted parts of our house that needed attention and donated unused clothing to a local charity. I reorganized my files and papers, and Amy refreshed our house with flowers and seasonal decorations. Our son Jonathan was home from Law School for Spring Break when the Covid-19 situation erupted and stayed home to finish his semester online. Because we were together, we scheduled daily walks. This program aided our fitness and renewed our connections with one another. We tested different recipes and cooked together, which further strengthened our family bond. Each day Jonathan selected an informational television program that fit his interests, and we watched it together. Amy and I took additional walks together and spent hours praying and discussing our future. Based on these discussions, we revised some plans, rejected others, and clarified the rest. We had not had such valuable conversations for years.

I also decided to make a list of "significant" goals that needed attention. I wanted to elevate these "purpose-related" goals. I used the first few days to reorder my reading schedule. I selected several books with the information I needed for my purpose and studied them carefully. I took notes of ideas that would help me fulfill my purpose. Because I need good health to accomplish my purpose, I increased my running to six miles a day and worked up to 100 push-ups per work out. I monitored my food and focused on protein and vegetables. I worked on an improved plan for my Choose Greatness television show and researched new topics. I participated in several online conferences and kept in contact with key leaders who were involved with our purpose. I spent more intentional time in prayer and Bible study and was rewarded with a renewed awareness of Gods indescribable presence and awesome peace. And I did one more thing: I wrote the book you are reading.

This combination of "ordinary" goals and "significant" goals formed a balance that moved us forward. The ordinary goals smoothed some of the rough places that needed attention, and the significant lifegoals advanced the fulfillment of our purpose.

Our unexpected time at home provided us with a special opportunity for growth and improvement. This growth prepared us to pursue our purpose more effectively. The simple lesson is that you need to go deep to be great. Significant lifegoals help you go deep.

The Psychiatrist Who Wanted to Be Alone

Carl Jung was an early pioneer in psychology and the founder of the analytical school of psychotherapy. He spent his career in his native Switzerland and was a close friend and follower of Sigmund Freud. Jung has been enormously influential, not only in psychology but in popular culture. He is referenced in thousands of books, the subject of several movies, and an influence on two video games. He is on the cover of the iconic Beatles album, *Sgt. Pepper's Lonely Hearts Club Band*, and the inspiration for some of the music of pop legend David Bowie.

Jung broke with Freud and started a school of psychotherapy that continues today. His books are still carefully studied in Universities and Schools of Medicine throughout the world, almost sixty years after his death at 85. One of the most used psychological tests in common use, the Myers-Briggs Type Indicator is based on his concepts. He invented the idea of having a "complex" as well as creating the modern understanding of "introvert" and "extrovert." He wrote so deeply and effectively about the human personality that his ideas are still being discussed decades after his death.

I am not telling you about Carl Jung as an endorsement of his teaching but as an example of a man who accomplished amazing things because he learned the art of "going deep." As Jung's career and influence expanded, he made a crucial decision that kept him on the track to greatness in his profession. He built a tower. *The* tower was a simple, isolated structure near his home in Switzerland. It had no electricity and no heat. It was warmed by a fireplace and lit by candles. It had only one purpose, to give him a place to think long and hard about the human condition. Jung realized that the constant stimulation of his busy life was interfering with his ability to think and imagine. He understood that for his influence to spread wide, he had to go deep. The tower gave him a place to stop, think, plan, and reflect. The ideas that startled and moved other people came from his commitment to go deep in his private tower. Our time of enforced coronavirus separation and isolation gave us a chance to "go deep." Let me encourage you to take advantage of your opportunities to learn the skill of deep and powerful thought. You can accelerate your drive to greatness by adding depth and understanding to your life. Sometimes you need to "embrace the quiet" and "empower the pause." You need the time to "go deep." Continual stimulation and constant entertainment can rob you of time to think and grow, so you need to learn this new skill set for significance and success as you determine your true lifegoals.

- Learn to use your time to examine your life.

- Learn to listen to God and meditate on His purpose.

- Learn to analyze your relationships so you can understand and love people better.

- Learn to make better decisions.

- Learn how to see the truth in every situation.

- Learn how to pursue SIGNIFICANT lifegoals.

The Bible says in Psalm 46:10, *"...Be still and know that I am God. I will be exalted among the nations; I will be exalted in the earth"* You learn significance in the quiet places in your life.

Satisfying Goals

Inner satisfaction is an indicator that you are following your life- goals. I have already written about the peace and calm that support you when you are on the right track. Inner satisfaction is an additional sign you are in alignment with your purpose. A sense of satisfaction is the comfortable awareness that your life fits your purpose. When I enjoy a chocolate milkshake or appreciate a movie, I experience a feeling of happiness. When I receive a message from someone who was helped by one of my seminars or benefited from the content of one of my books, I experience a sense of satisfaction. There is nothing wrong with the milkshake (in moderation) or my interaction with an interesting movie, but the satisfaction that arises from the fulfillment of my purpose to improve the lives of other people through the application of Gods principles is deeper and more powerful than "ordinary" experiences.

The Leader Who Wasn't Embarrassed

I was speaking at a Christian rally in a sports arena. Most of the people attending had participated in a sales and motivational convention the previous two days and had stayed for the rally on Sunday. Many of the business leaders who had guided the convention were also in the Sunday service.

After a period of inspirational music, I gave a simple message explaining how to enter a relationship with Jesus Christ. I was almost finished when a man on the front row stood up. The crowd watched in quiet curiosity as he walked to the edge of the stage. I stopped speaking and looked down. I knew the man. He was one of the leaders from the business convention. He had spoken the previous day, and everyone recognized him.

A hush settled on the arena as I knelt on the stage and, using the microphone in my hand, asked him why he had walked to the front. He answered that God had touched his heart, and he wanted to make a public commitment to Jesus Christ as his Lord and Savior. He was so moved that he could not wait for the public invitation to respond at the end of the service. I led him in prayer, then stood and asked if anyone else in the arena wanted to join him at the front in a public commitment to Christ. Fifteen thousand people swarmed to the front in a powerful expression of spiritual response. It was deep, stirring, and genuine.

I have had many moments of temporary happiness. I have enjoyed experiences that stimulated and refreshed me. But that moment in the arena at the end of the service brought me a more profound sense of satisfaction because I had accomplished my purpose. I was happy, but I was also content with the knowledge that thousands of people had received the help they needed for a better life.

The Ham Sandwich

I was speaking in Dallas, Texas, at a convention hosted by my friend and mentor, Dexter Yager, the Amway business owner, you have already met in this book. I was visiting him in his hotel suite when he asked me if I wanted something to eat. I looked at the menu and saw a cheeseburger option. I was about to order the cheeseburger when Dexter said he was going to have a ham sandwich and asked if I wanted one as well.

I thought it would be more polite to accept his suggestion, so I agreed to order the ham sandwich. Forty minutes later, the food arrived, and we paused our meeting to eat. The ham sandwich was good, but I felt disappointed at missing the cheeseburger.

Less than an hour after our meal, I was walking through the hotel lobby and spotted a restaurant. On impulse, I entered and ordered a cheeseburger to take to my room. When the sandwich came, I took it upstairs to my room and rapidly devoured it. I was not hungry because I had just eaten the ham sandwich but forced myself to eat the cheeseburger. The combination of both sandwiches in a short time overwhelmed my digestive system, and I was sick with indigestion for the rest of the evening. I spent a miserable night, regretting my eating choices.

There are two lessons here. First, you should be clear about what you want in life. If you want a cheeseburger, you should eat a cheeseburger. The second lesson is that if you try to indulge yourself with an abundance of "ordinary" goals, you will have moments of enjoyment but will miss the satisfaction that comes when you focus on lifegoals. I liked the taste of both sandwiches, but too much food was not "satisfying." You are not meant to live on a diet of ordinary goals. Too many of them can overwhelm you. You need to balance your ordinary goals (which are not bad) with life-purpose goals that bring the nourishing satisfaction of fulfilling that purpose.

The Map

Amy fully supported me when I left graduate school and launched a career in public speaking. We used what little money we had to travel to various locations for our meetings. Once we stayed "on the road' for fifteen weeks, sleeping in our car and using interstate rest areas for bathroom stops. We were happy, wildly in love (we still are), and committed to the pursuit of our purpose.

We finished one seminar on a Thursday evening in Ohio and left to speak at a church service in Florida on Sunday. We decided to drive two hours after the conclusion of the seminar and stopped for the night in Cincinnati. As we were preparing to leave the next morning, Amy asked me how long it would take us to drive to Ft. Lauderdale, Florida, for our next engagement. I said that it could not be "that far" and that we would drive that day to Atlanta, stop for another night, and continue to Ft. Lauderdale the next day. I assured her that we would arrive in Florida rested and ready for the service on Sunday.

We reached Atlanta and found a hotel. Because I had told Amy that we had "plenty of time," we slept late and departed for Ft. Lauderdale at noon. As we drove (and drove and drove), I realized that it was much further to Ft. Lauderdale that I had assumed, and we were going to need to drive all day and into the next morning to fulfill our responsibility. We were somewhere in South Georgia when Amy became angry. Amy is a sweet, generous, loving person, but she had crossed a line. She told me that she was tired and unhappy with our intense drive. Amy had trusted my judgment and wanted to know how I had been so mistaken about the distance. She then asked me a key question, "didn't you look at a map"? I said that I had not consulted a map but had relied on my estimate of the distance, which I admitted, was a guess based on no facts or research. She was shocked and asked me why I had planned a trip without a map. I had no answer.

We arrived in Ft. Lauderdale after two a.m. and found our hotel with difficulty. By the time we checked in, unpacked, and were ready for bed, it was 4 a.m., and we were exhausted. We conducted the service, then went to lunch. After lunch, we returned to our hotel room. Once in the hotel, I apologized to Amy, asked her forgiveness, and promised that I would never make again make the mistake of traveling without a map. My foolish stubbornness had hurt my wife and diminished our ability to fulfill our commitments.

Think of the word MAP in two ways.

First, the word MAP can mean **Meaning and Purpose.** Your meaning and purpose are the "map" that guides you and determines your decisions.

Second, the word MAP can mean: **Mastering All Plans.** Understanding this can help you remember that all your plans are structured by your "masterplan," which is based on your commitment to your purpose.

When I chose to travel to Florida without a map, that decision inserted uncertainty into our trip. We were unable to make accurate decisions and almost missed our meeting. The lack of a map put us at the mercy of our circumstances. A map would have protected our schedule, lowered our stress, and given us the right tool to meet our goal. When you "Master All Plans" (MAP) through your purpose and allow your "Mission and Purpose" (MAP) to guide you, then you more easily stay on the right path. When you neglect your "map," you risk losing your way.

The Four Average People

Many people choose an over-cautious, fear-filled approach to life without the sensational life goals that give energy and inspiration. Let me show you four hypothetical examples that represent the types of individuals who avoid their mission and miss their purpose.

Tommy Typical

Tommy Typical is the person who prefers a safe "middle of the road" life. Tommy goes to school, gets a job, starts a family, buys, or rents a home, spends decades in a boring routine, takes a yearly vacation, retires and dies. Tommy leaves no mark, creates no legacy, and ends without any significant impact. There are moments when he feels the itch to be more and do more, but he never explores what that itch means. Tommy numbs himself with media entertainment and ignores the need to expand and grow.

Tommy is probably a "nice" person and cares for his family. He deserves credit for providing for those who depend on him and is often honest and dependable. But Tommy misses his mission and fails to accomplish his purpose. He lives his entire life with a vague sense of disappointment.

Mary Mediocre

Mary Mediocre chooses to stay in the lane she began as a child. She never questions her direction and follows the "path of least resistance."

She walks through whatever door opens and easily allows other people to determine her direction. She moves through life with no clear plan, and her focus is mostly on maintaining her position. Mary, like Tommy, is occasionally aware of a higher purpose but never develops the depth that could give her the insights that could lead her out of her "ordinary" mediocre life and place her onto a path to her purpose.

This does not mean that the "ordinary" experiences of life are signs of failure. Many "ordinary" things are normal parts of life. But when a person accepts the "ordinary" and surrenders to the mediocre, something vital is suppressed. Life becomes dull and uninteresting. Mary Ordinary is not a "bad person"; she just never leaves her "ordinary" lane and ventures onto the superhighway of her purpose. She misses the electrifying energy of her true mission.

Davy Dull

Davy stopped developing when he finished school and remained stuck at that mental and emotional point for the rest of his life. He read no more books and interacted with no new people. Davy settled into a routine and never considered whether any other way was better. Davy's ability to think rusted through lack of use, and he never looked at new ideas. Once Davy learned how to do something, he never opened his mind to anything better. He believed that the way he had always done something was the way he should still do it. Davy never considered different possibilities and never challenged his patterns and habits. He stayed stuck on one track his whole life. Davy was dull because he never improved and never grew. Davy was the same every year. Because of this, he lost any desire for greater things. He lived so long in his "dullness" that he lost the ability to envision a future filled with his purpose. Although he, at times, felt that something was "missing," he always ignored his "purpose- signal" and remained dull and unmoved.

Lucy Limited

Lucy started with dreams and goals, but the difficulties and disappointments of life wore her down. Lucy is likable and enthusiastic but insecure about her ability to succeed. She harbors hidden doubts that she reveals to no one. These doubts cause her to accept artificial limits. She creates her limits because she thinks she can only go so far. Her self-created limits keep her from stretching and expanding. Whenever she experiences a small success, she feels that she does not deserve her success and pulls back. When someone compliments her, she feels embarrassed and gives reasons why she is not as good as they think. Lucy wants to live with purpose and focus but believes herself unworthy. Her self-doubt erodes her confidence and makes her hesitant to pursue new opportunities. Her fear of failure inhibits her ability to make quick decisions, and she often misses moments when she could have moved forward. Because Lucy believes she is too limited to rise higher, she fails to try. The older she gets, the more she accepts her limitations. Lucy gradually gives up her dreams and surrenders her goals. Her self-limitations create real limitations, and she misses her mission. There are moments when she remembers her longing for something more, but eventually, that fades into an empty life.

Four New People

It is possible to fight the negative forces of defeat and disappointment. It is possible to rise above the routine mediocrity of life and blaze like a star. It is possible to fulfill your purpose.
With the right commitment and attitude, you can become one of the following types.

Tommy Terrific

Tommy Typical can become Tommy Terrific when he chooses to break out of the typical patterns of most people and launch into his mission orbit. Tommy can refuse to remain in his "typical" world and travel into new worlds of possibility. Tommy can seize his opportunities and rise to his challenges. Tommy can surprise his friends and family by choosing intelligent risk over the fear of failure. Tommy can climb the ladder of new goals until he reaches the heights of success. Tommy can become "terrific" when he finds his mission.

Mary Memorable

Mary Mediocre can become Mary Memorable when she decides to leave the "ordinary," safe routines of life and swim in streams of possibility. When she masters the ordinary, she can then move on to the remarkable. Mary has already shown that she can operate in the "ordinary" parts of life; she can then use those skills to add new skills so she can advance toward her purpose. The more remarkable things she accomplishes, the more satisfied she becomes with her direction. Her fulfillment deepens as her mission unfolds. She becomes memorable.

Davy Dynamic

Davy changes from dull to dynamic when he decides to burst from his shell and explore new options. Davy reads new books, meets new people, accepts unique challenges, learns further information, seizes new opportunities, and stretches to a new level. Davy is suddenly more attractive to other people and attracts successful individuals who want to help him.

Davy explodes with fresh ideas and is willing to try new methods. His income increases, and his opportunities multiply. Davy is excited to wake up each morning and advance into the day.

His days of dullness are over because he decided to be dynamic. Davy has discovered his purpose, and the power of that purpose has filled his life. Davy is motivated to help other people. His example is an inspiration.

Lucy Limitless

Lucy moved from limited to limitless when she decided to disbelieve her fear and trust her dreams. When Lucy pushed out of her limited life, her confidence soared. She was no longer dependent on the approval of other people because she now has proof of her accomplishments.

Lucy found her purpose and pursued it with courage and conviction. Her life was now organized around her mission. Her time was full of meaningful actions that contributed to the welfare of other people. Her fear that her internal limitations would keep her from reaching her lifegoals was gone. Her fear has been replaced by a fierce belief in her ability to accomplish her calling.

The Choice

The one connecting thread among all these examples is choice. You decide who you will be. You decide what you will do. You decide what you will risk. You choose whether to be:

- **Tommy Typical** or **Tommy Terrific**

- **Mary Mediocre** or **Mary Memorable**

- **Davy Dull** or **Davy Dynamic**

- **Lucy Limited** or **Lucy Limitless**

Why You Should Improve Yourself

I believe that when God gives you your purpose, it is your choice to accept it or reject it. If you accept your purpose, it is also your choice to make yourself into your best version so you can more easily fulfill that purpose. Often you are told to accept yourself the way you are and that you do not need to change. But there is a crucial difference between your WORTH and your USEFULNESS. You have automatic worth as God's special creation, but you only have value when you are useful.
Dr. Neil Postman was a university professor and respected cultural commentator who specialized in contemporary media issues. His book, Amusing Ourselves to Death (1985), which warned about too high a dependence on entertainment, is one of the most influential books on the effect of media published in the last thirty-five years. Postman wrote in Building a Bridge to the Eighteenth Century, that all good in life is engineered by men and women who committed themselves to improvement and used their advances to serve their society. Postman believed that greatness comes from improving the lives of other people, and the foundation for that is the commitment to improve yourself first. When you read the writings of eighteenth-century leaders, they all write about self-improvement as preparation for usefulness. Alexander Hamilton was born out of wedlock in Charlestown in the British Leeward Islands in the Caribbean. He was orphaned as a child and informally "adopted" by a wealthy merchant who sent him, as a teenager, to New York City to pursue his education. His foster father instilled in him a determination for 'improvement" that guided his life and career.

Hamilton joined the American revolutionary army and worked hard to develop useable skills in organization and communication. These skills led him to a position as a senior aide to General George Washington. His drive for continual improvement had prepared him when Washington was seeking someone to assist him. The relationship with Washington created opportunities after the war that gave Hamilton even higher positions of service. Eventually, he became the first United States Secretary of the Treasury.

This was a lofty height for a boy who started as an orphan and social outcast, but he reached it because of his unrelenting commitment to improvement and creating value. At each critical point in his career, he emerged as the man with the knowledge and skills to accomplish what needed to be done.

If young Hamilton had believed that he should accept himself "just the way he was," then his astonishing rise to power would probably have never happened. His improvements made him valuable when such a man was needed. Therefore, you should never accept yourself 'for the way you are" but instead improve yourself. Great opportunities are available for people who "better" themselves and create value for others.

The Man Who Wanted to Help

Early in my relationship with Dexter Yager, the important mentor who guided my development, I was asked to meet with him at his home. I arrived, curious, and waited for him to start our meeting. Dexter walked into the room, sat down, and thanked me for coming on short notice. He said that he wanted my input with a situation then explained the details. When he finished, I agreed to do my best to help but wondered why he had not asked me by phone. That question was answered when Dexter left and returned with a couple. He said that the couple was having a challenge in their marriage and had agreed to meet with us.

Dexter thought it would be more effective if I met with the couple in person.

The couple was positive and receptive, and we formulated a plan to help their situation. We prayed, and they left. After they had left, Dexter thanked me and said that he was grateful I had invested my time.

A few months later, I spoke with the couple and was happy that they had followed the plan, and their marriage was in recovery. I reported my conversation to Dexter. All of this happened during a difficult time when my organization was facing a severe financial challenge. I needed support and could have asked my wealthy friend for help during my visit, but I thought that my focus should be on assisting the struggling couple. Because of the success of the plan, we formulated together, Dexter asked me to help other individuals with marital and spiritual needs. Soon, my relationship with Dexter deepened, and he arranged for me to speak to dozens of conventions. I channeled the speaking fees I received, and the amounts received for the books and audios I made available at the conferences into our ministry organization, and our financial dilemma was solved.

Once when Amy and I were discussing the events of that year, she produced an insight that explained how our problems had been solved. She said that when I focused on helping meet the needs of others rather than getting my own needs met, I became VALUABLE. It was the value I brought when Dexter asked for spiritual insights that deepened our relationship. It was the added value that made him want to include me as a speaker. And that value was based on the IMPROVEMENTS I had made in myself.

I had spent years reading and studying to increase my skills in speaking and counseling. I spent long sessions in training with one of the top counseling experts in America. I studied counseling in my master's degree program and had had thousands of hours of experience in public and private communication. If I had never grown, expanded, or improved, I would have had little of value to contribute.

The philosopher, John Locke, wrote, "The improvement of understanding is for two ends: first, our increase of knowledge; secondly, to enable us to deliver that knowledge to others." God guided and used my development to bless other people. That is how purpose works. I am sure there are people who know more and understand people better than I do but God used what little experience I had to create improvement for someone else.

Marie Curie, the only woman to win the Nobel Prize twice, said, "You cannot build a better world without improving individuals. To that end, each of us must work for his improvement and, at the same time, share a general responsibility for all humanity, our duty being to aid those to who we think we can be most useful."

Winston Churchill said, "Continuous effort—not strength and intelligence—is the key to unlocking our potential." This quote teaches that your improvement has a purpose. It is to help you fulfill your purpose and not to increase your ego. The modern idea that all your effort should go into making yourself better is not enough. You should use your attempt to make yourself better so your purpose can succeed for the benefit of other people.

It's not about you.

CHAPTER 6

The

I HOPE you now understand how your goals fit the advancement of your purpose. When you grasp this, then you are ready for a "goal explosion" to rock your world and push you out of your "comfort zone" The most important thing to remember is the difference between "ordinary goals" that are a part of your regular life and the significant "lifegoals" that carry you forward. "Ordinary goals" are necessary for you to function. You need "lifegoals" for your purpose to advance.

The Hut in Haiti

I was in Haiti to speak at a leadership conference. I was met at the airport and driven to a location two hours away. When we arrived, I was escorted to a cabin that was little more than a hut on the beach. The cabin had one small room with a bed and one chair. A bathroom with a shower and toilet completed the accommodations.

The heat and humidity smothered me (it was in July), and the cabin had no air conditioning. The only relief from the heat came from a ceiling fan and one partially opened window with a screen to keep out mosquitoes. The one pleasant aspect of the site was the proximity of the ocean, about twenty yards away. I changed clothes and waited.

Soon a man knocked on the door. I opened it, and he told me that he was there to escort me to a conference center where I would give my first presentation. We walked under tall, swaying palm trees and followed a path lined with thick shrubs filled with brilliant scarlet flowers.

When we reached the meeting site, I saw a long line of men and women entering the building. I was taken to the back and guided to an area near the stage. After some announcements, I was introduced and gave my seminar. I was escorted back to the hut and left there for the night. Even with the excessive heat and humidity, I was tired enough to fall asleep quickly. I woke early the next morning to brilliant sunshine reflecting off the ocean and a mixture of the sounds of crashing waves and the calls of loud, tropical birds.

I walked to an open-air building for breakfast, where I met with the team who were coordinating the conference. We enjoyed a breakfast of fresh fruit and toast and discussed plans for the remainder of the meeting. After breakfast, I returned to the hut. I had several uninterrupted hours and was uncertain what to do. I decided to read a book but soon had a sense that I was supposed to do something different. I replaced the book with a notebook and pen, settled into the chair, and said a prayer. I asked God to show me anything about my purpose that I was missing. Then I waited.

For the first hour, nothing happened, and I almost quit, but then I remembered a conversation I had had with an unusual man several years before. E. Stanley Jones was a Methodist missionary leader in India whose friendship with Mohandas Gandhi led him to develop a lecture series that explained the Christian faith in a way that showed respect to the Hindus and Buddhists without compromising the message of Christ. Jones became famous in India for his efforts to communicate his faith and delivered lectures on the subject to the leaders of India. The response was sensational. Thousands attended the talks, and Jones became a national figure. He wrote a book about his experiences, *The Christ of the Indian Road*, sold over a million copies in less than a year. When he returned to the United States, he was a celebrity sought out by numerous religious and political leaders and had private meetings with the President of the United States.

I met Dr. Jones when he visited Asbury College, where I was a student. Jones was a graduate of Asbury and made periodic visits to the campus to lecture.

After one of his speeches, I stayed after everyone had left the auditorium to meet the famous man. He had a gentle spirit and made me feel welcome and appreciated, although I was a student he had never met. I asked Dr. Jones to describe the most important thing he had learned about spiritual leadership. He replied that my question had an easy answer. He explained that many years before, when he was engaged in multiple ministries in India, he encountered an unexpected problem. He was traveling extensively and speaking continually. While involved in the lectures, he tried to carve out time each day for writing. He was receiving visits from many of the influential leaders of India who wanted his opinion on numerous issues. All this exhausted him. He became confused and had difficulty deciding on priorities. His health began to suffer.

It was at this point that he discovered a technique that saved him. He reorganized his morning schedule so he could spend the first hour alone. He used this time to sit quietly and reflect on the coming day. This practice grew into what he called his "listening post." He decided that, instead of asking God for things, he would simply listen and allow time for God to speak to him.

This practice produced powerful results. Jones began to see solutions to problems that had baffled him. He felt a strong sense of calm envelop him. His decisions became clear and evident as he sensed the right direction. He perceived strategies that would improve his relationships. All of this happened because he just listened to God.

After I remembered my experience with E. Stanley Jones, I decided to make the Haitian beach hut my listening post. I opened the window, turned on the fan, sat in the chair, and waited. Nothing happened. For an hour, I anticipated remarkable results, but none came. When the first hour expired, I decided to wait one more hour, and if nothing happened, I would stop and spend the rest of the afternoon with my book.

At the end of the second hour, I thought that I had wasted my time when I became aware of a change. I felt an overwhelming sense of God's presence. Suddenly a blazing clarity entered my mind, and I understood answers to struggles I had had for years. As I sat, surprising insights filled my thoughts, and I saw a map of my future.

While I waited, I became conscious of several mistakes I had made. I saw the consequences of my choices and realized that my goals had become confused. I received a new vision of my purpose and saw how I was neglecting the goals that could make it happen. For the next two and a half hours, I was flooded with ideas that advanced my purpose. Then, just as suddenly as it started, it ended. I felt a wave of contentment and satisfaction.

My purpose was renewed.

I am not telling you that you need to repeat my experience to understand your purpose. But you can still benefit from the clarity that comes when you stop the frenzied busyness of your life and listen to the signals all around you. You can still use a "listening post" to create a calm moment when your mind is open to the ideas and direction you need. Sometimes you need to stop to move forward. My time in the Haitian hut reminded me of how easy it is to pursue the wrong goals. In your haste to improve your life, you can lose sight of your lifegoals and replace them with goals that seem urgent but are not connected to your ultimate purpose.

The Power of the Right Goals

When you pursue the right goals, they become beacons that shed light on your path. Look at the following list. Each point reveals how the right goals can get you to your destination.

The Right Goals Give You Guidance

When you know where you are going and why you are going there, it is easier to decide what to do with your time. You can make schedules based on those goals that advance you toward your destination.

The Man with Too Much to Do

known James for five years and had always appreciated his drive and ambition. James was dependable and consistently finished projects correctly and on schedule. He arrived on time and explained that he was juggling four assignments and could not decide which one to prioritize. James said that all four had value and potential. He liked each project equally and enjoyed working with the different teams. The challenge was that he did not have the time or energy to do all four. James did not want to disappoint anyone and was uncertain what to do. He knew he should eliminate at least one project but could not choose which one. I asked him to describe the projects in detail and tell me what results each would produce when completed.

When he finished, I told him the story about the consultant who showed his clients a cardboard box and asked, "What's in your box?". I then asked him, "What's in your box?" He thought for a moment, looked up, and said, "the reason for everything I do is simple. My brother died of leukemia when he was thirteen. I was nine and remember making a promise at his funeral that someday I would make enough money to donate millions of dollars to research to find a cure for cancer in children."

As I listened to his story, his eyes glistened with tears. The memory of his brother brought him to a moment of crystal-clear clarity. He looked at me and said, "making enough money to keep that promise is what is in my box."

We sat in silence for several minutes. I respected the grief he still felt and gave him time to continue. When he nodded that he was ready to resume the conversation, I pointed out that the contents of his "box" had already made his decision for him. His purpose determined his goals. When I finished, he said that he had added three of the projects to his crowded schedule because friends had proposed them, and he did not want to "let them down." They were small but time- consuming projects that would give him little money. The fourth project, if successful, would pay his expenses, engineering fee and give him a bonus of $120,000 if the job were completed on schedule. That schedule would be impossible if he continued the other projects.

James is a generous man who tries to help people. He is active in his church and volunteers to cut the grass on the church grounds each week. His weakness is that he dislikes saying no when asked to do something. This weakness had caused him to accept more work than he could handle. When he remembered his purpose, the next goal decision was easy. He canceled the three small projects so he could focus on the project that contributed to his purpose.

The Goal Thread

The story of James and his over-commitment is an example of what I call "the goal thread." This is defined as a connective thread that runs from your purpose to your goals then back to you. Imagine a box that contains your purpose. A strong thread leaves the box and connects it to the goals that are then connected to your purpose. If you focus on the right goals, they will lead you along that thread back to your purpose box. The thread gives guidance. When you evaluate your goals and decisions, you should always pick the goals that follow the thread. This process helps you transfer your energy from the trivial to the important.

The NASCAR Champion

I grew up with a man whose father owned a coal mine. When his father died, he inherited the mining operation and developed it into a multi-million-dollar business. Harry sold the mine and used the money to enter the world of thoroughbred horse racing. He bought 571 acres of rolling bluegrass land near Lexington, Kentucky, and built a horse breeding farm with spectacular barns and a 28,000 square foot home. My friend worked hard to establish himself in the thoroughbred industry and received an invitation to enter a horse in the English Derby. When his horse won, he and his wife, Judy, were presented to Queen Elizabeth II of Great Britain. Harry told me that even this proud moment did not compare with his three NASCAR championships.

When Harry's father died, he also inherited a NASCAR racing team. Harry was fascinated by horse racing but was in love with car racing. He poured his passion into the NASCAR team and built it into one of the premier NASCAR units in the United States. Harry's racing group won with the Daytona 500 in 1980 with driver Buddy Baker and won the Daytona 500 again in 1983 and 1984 with driver Cale Yarborough. Amy and I once spent a weekend with Harry and Judy at their home, Shadowlawn Farm. We enjoyed excellent Kentucky hospitality and visited Keeneland Raceway, considered by many, the most beautiful track in America. During our visit Harry and I talked about the town where we had grown up and the many people, we both knew. Harry had started a relationship with Christ a few years before, and much of our conversation centered on his spiritual growth.

When our talk paused, I asked him about his NASCAR championships. I wanted to know if there were any "secrets" to his success. His answer surprised me. He said that the most important thing he had done was to assemble a highly motivated and skilled team who believed in their "mission" to win the race. It was not this statement that surprised me, but what came next. Harry said that three things were crucial to the performance of the team.

First, they had had to work in unison, with no division and no distractions. Each member of the team was equally important, and each one focused on their part of the process. Second, they had to work fast. They were competing with other teams whose sole purpose was to be faster than any other group. Top speed was essential and non-negotiable. And third, (the part that surprised me) was the absolute necessity of great tires. The tires were the critical contact between the car and the track. Each tire had to perform with minimal friction and maximum traction. If a tire underperformed, then the race was lost. The tires provided the grip that kept the car from skidding and kept the car moving toward the finish line.

Harry asked me if I had noticed how often (and how fast) a team changes tires during a race. When I said I had seen what he described, he pointed out that that activity was often the difference between winning and losing. The cars all had expertly designed engines and highly skilled and motivated drivers. It was the tires that won the race.

The most important thing a tire does on any car is to "grip" the road. Without this gripping effect, the vehicle will lose control and slide to one side or the other. The tire also keeps the car going in the direction chosen by the driver.

The right goals are like tires. They enable you to "grip" the road as you travel toward the fulfillment of your purpose. If you ever perceive that you are following the wrong goals, then it is time to change the goals the way you change tires. The right goals keep you straight and allow you to move toward your mission. Your goals are your tires. Always remember, the right goals give you traction, stability, and help you avoid slippage. Always "check your tires" to be sure that you are investing your time and energy on goals that get you where you want to go.

The Pencil Distraction

Once in college I was engaged in completing a series of assignments and quizzes. Everything had to finished by a specific time. This experience was before the computer era, and I was supposed to use a pencil to mark my answers on quizzes attached to the assignments. I had bought ten pencils, but none were sharpened, so I left my room to find someone with a pencil sharpener. While looking for the pencil sharpener, I spoke with several students on my floor and forgot my reason for being out of the room. I talked and joked as we shared stories of our first day of classes. Eventually, I remembered the pencil sharpener and left to locate what I needed. When I returned to my room, the hour was over, and I had not even begun my studies. At that point, I decided to stop the plan and start the next night again, but when I started the following evening, I realized that I had only sharpened one pencil and needed to leave and search for another pencil sharpener. I was again distracted by other students and returned with no time left for study. Before you think that I was hopelessly stupid, I can tell you that after the second failure, I realized what I was doing wrong and changed my behavior. By the third night, I was ready with all my pencils sharpened. From that night, I completed all my assignments on time.

This type of situation is a common problem. Many people spend more time getting ready to work than they spend working. Often the long preparation time is an excuse to avoid the task. It is easy to substitute "busyness" for the real job and then wonder why so little gets done. After my failure on the second night, I realized that my goal was not to sharpen pencils; my goal was to complete my study assignments. When I focused on the right goal, I was able to stay on target to fulfill my mission. The right goals provided the "grip" I needed to keep on the track.

The Right Goals Grease Your Progress

The right goals ease your progress and accelerate your speed.

The Toboggan Disaster

Early in our marriage, we invited Amy's sister to join us on vacation in the Great Smoky Mountains National Park. Amy's sister Pam flew in from New Jersey, we picked her up and left for the vacation. We checked into a hotel in Gatlinburg, Tennessee, and organized our plans for the week. When I asked the hotel receptionist for recommendations, she suggested that we drive the next day to a ski resort above the town and experience their toboggan ride. She said that it was modeled on similar rides in the European Alps and thought we would enjoy it. It was a blazingly hot summer day, and I asked how we could do a toboggan ride with no snow, and she said that they used special lubricants on the slide that enabled the sleds to move down the track.

The next morning, we drove to the ski resort, parked, and walked to the entrance to the toboggan ride. It was early, and we were the only customers. It was already sunny and sweltering, so we decided to ride once then leave. We climbed to the top of the toboggan run and waited. I noticed a woman on a side ladder spraying lubricant on the surface and watched as it ran down the track, which slowly covered the area where the toboggan would make contact. The attendant used the lubricant to replace the snow and ice that would have been present in the winter. I asked the attendant if the lubricant was safe, and she assured me that there was no danger. I rode first, and the lubricant performed well. I slid smoothly down the track, and, after two exhilarating minutes, I arrived at the bottom. My wife, Amy, was next and enjoyed the same smooth ride as I had.

My wife's sister was last, but before she boarded, the woman with the spray container stopped the ride to add more lubricant. When Pam started, we could see that she was traveling far faster than we had and watched with concern as she hurtled down the track. On the final curve, she hit a stretch of lubricant that had pooled on the surface, and her sled went airborne, left the track, and landed on the grass and bounced to a stop. We rushed to the site of the landing and found my young sister-in-law shaken, but with no serious harm. We immediately decided to end our tobogganing adventure and return to the town. As we drove down the mountain, we laughed and recovered from the scare we had experienced.

The right, strategic goals are the "lubricant" that speeds up your journey. The lubricant on the toboggan track caused instant acceleration and succeeded in shortening our descent to the finish line. The right goals do the same. They accelerate your progress and create momentum toward your purpose. The opposite is also true. If there had been no added lubricant on the track, we would still have made it to the bottom, but the trip would have been slow and difficult. If you spend time and energy on goals that do not fit your best plan, it is like trying to make progress on a dry track. The friction created by wrong goals or unworthy goals will slow your speed. You may still arrive at your destination but be exhausted by the unnecessary effort.

The Lost Election

One of the most unusual elections I entered was the one I lost. I was a junior in college when I decided to run for the incoming freshman class sponsor. The office I was interested in required a senior to coordinate activities for the new class and serve as their representative with the college administration. If elected, I would be responsible for planning the coming year for the new class. If I won the election, it would require multiple meetings and a significant investment of time.

My friends were surprised when I chose to run because I was away every weekend speaking at churches and public events. They knew that my passion was communicating God's success principles to as many people as possible and could not understand how this passion fit the job I was seeking. The comments of my friends created doubt, and I began to question my decision. They were right that my heart was firmly engaged in my speaking opportunities, but I was intrigued and curious about the possibilities of the elective office. I soon found that the campaign divided my attention and distracted me from my weekend schedule. I tried to balance the responsibilities of both commitments but only succeeded in adding to my challenges. I wanted to win the election but felt continual conflict. I struggled emotionally to reconcile my two directions but only succeeded in creating more struggle. The campaign began to interfere with my preparation for the speaking engagements, and my speaking engagements interfered with my campaign.

On the day of the election, I voted, attended class, and waited. I joined other students in the college auditorium that evening to hear the results. Other offices, such as student body president, were in contention, and several winners were announced before my result. I sat, anxious, and concerned as the current student body president read the results for my election. I lost and was very disappointed. Dozens of friends and supporters consoled me, but the most revealing comments came from students who had not voted for me. They all said the same thing. They liked me, and some had even considered voting for me, but each said that they voted against me because they knew of my commitment to spread the Christian message and were aware of my extensive speaking schedule. They believed that my heart was in my growing ministry, and they thought that the demands of "my heart" would eventually interfere with my performance in the office if elected. They thought that I would be too distracted to do a good job.

The more I was confronted with these comments, the more I realized that the people who had not voted for me were right. I had almost sacrificed my primary purpose for something good, but that did not support that essential purpose. My disappointment changed to relief. Losing the election saved my mission. This was my first experience with the life-principle that states, "the good is the enemy of the best."

I could have undoubtedly "done good" as the leader and coordinator of the incoming class, but that was not my primary mission. If I had won the election, it would have detoured me off my main path. I also learned the lesson that the wrong goal (even if that goal is for something good and helpful) only slows you down.

When you use your time, energy, and resources to pursue goals that are unconnected to your purpose, it is like trying to ride a toboggan down a track without lubricant. The friction will wear you out. It takes more time, energy, and resources to follow the wrong goals because you are dragging against the friction of your detour. It is always better to throw yourself fully into your mission. The "lubrication" of the right "lifegoals" will grease your tracks and help you fly to the finish line.

CHAPTER 7
The Desires of Your Heart

There is a powerful statement in the Bible about desire. The verses in Psalm 37, 3-4, read, *"Trust in the Lord and do good; dwell in the land and enjoy safe pasture. Take delight in the Lord, and He will give you the desires of your heart!'* These verses make clear that God cares about your safety, security, and "the desires of your heart." These verses are not a blanket promise to give you anything you want. This statement about desire is conditional on delighting in the Lord, which implies that your desires are in sync with what pleases and honors him. These desires are the deepest motivations that guide your life. They are the inner springs that nourish your life.

But what is desire and where does it come from? Many people think of desire only in sexual terms and see it as an expression of romance or lust. 27 Hebrew words are translated "desire" in the Old Testament of the Bible. All of them carry the meaning of longing for something with intense focus. The terms also have a root meaning of looking at something with favor, pleasure, and delight. The words all convey the idea of deep emotional attachment. Desire is simply something you want with all your heart and mind with an intense determination to possess it.

The Greek word *epithumia* is translated desire in the New Testament and means to crave something with a resolve to get it. Both the Hebrew and Greek words can be translated as "lust" or "desire" You can "lust" sexually after a person (you can also "lust after" your husband or wife, which is right and proper), but you can also "lust" after a deeper relationship with God. You can "lust" after financial freedom or "lust" after someone else's possessions that do not belong to you. The words are neutral. It is what you are "lusting after" that makes it good or bad.

All improvement in life is based on something you desire. Your desire is the fuel for your engine. It is important to note that not everything is a "desire." Many things in life seem like desires because you want them, but they are only things you are interested in or curious about, not things you desire with intensity and determination. You may want to see a new movie or try a different menu item in your favorite restaurant, but these do not rise to the level of true desire. You want them but can live happily without them.

A "desire" is defined by intensity and longing. It is something that connects to your deepest needs. A true desire is something that supplies a missing piece of your life, something for which you are willing to fight. These are the "desires of your heart." I dated numerous young women in college. I enjoyed their company and appreciated their qualities, but none became the "desire of my heart" until I met and dated Amy.

The Man I Ignored

You have already read the story of how God directed me to Amy. You probably recall my excitement when I saw her early on the morning of my first day of summer school. But I want you to know more about the story. Two weeks after my "morning of destiny" when I saw Amy coming through the dawn mist, I knew I wanted to ask her for a date, but when I asked a friend how I should proceed, he told me that she was already dating a young man in the graduate school. I investigated and found that I knew the young man. He was "a nice guy," ambitious and appealing to young women, which included Amy. I also discovered that he and Amy had started dating when summer school began, and their friends thought it already "seemed serious."

At first, I was confused. My surprise reaction when I had seen Amy two months before in the college cafeteria had led me to believe that God intended something special. I still remembered my overwhelming sense that Amy (who I barely knew at the time) was the woman I wished I were marrying. Now she was in a relationship with someone else.

I then made one of the most vital decisions of my life. I decided to pursue Amy regardless of her involvement with anyone else. My opportunity to pursue Amy came one afternoon when I went to the college grill for a snack. When I entered the room, I saw Amy and the graduate student at a table by a window. All thought of food fled my mind as I walked to their table. There was an empty seat beside Amy, and I sat down. I politely nodded to the young man then engaged Amy in a conversation for several minutes. I noticed the young man glaring at me but ignored him and concentrated on Amy. To my relief, she responded positively. She seemed amused, and I noticed a "twinkle" in her eyes as we talked. I told Amy how great it was to see her and left.

Two days later, I learned that she had ended her relationship with the graduate student. I asked her out the next day.

One month after our first date, Amy informed me that she wanted to pause our relationship. She said she wanted to focus on her studies. She told me this while we were sitting on a bench in a beautiful park, in the shade of enormous mature trees. I listened, acknowledged her need to study then told her I would pick her up for dinner at 7 o'clock. She stared at me for a few moments then said she would be ready at 7. We have been together since that moment.

She later told me that she had offered to "pause" our relationship, although she wanted it to continue but was afraid it might not work out. Our relationship developed and deepened for the rest of the year until I knew I wanted to marry her. She had become "the desire of my heart." My interest had increased until interest became a desire. From the encounter at the college grill to the moment on the park bench to the day I drove her to a quiet spot by a gurgling stream to ask her to marry me, everything that happened was an expression of growing desire.

The same is true of your growing awareness of your life-purpose.

Why You Want What You Want

My desire for a relationship with Amy illustrates the power that desire brings to your life. It is sometimes difficult to explain the attraction you feel toward another person, but you know the attraction is real. There are unconscious forces that drive your desire that are beneath the surface but exert tremendous influence. The good news is that it is possible to uncover and understand these motivations. Here are four things that are core creators of the desires that drive you and offer clues to the discovery of your purpose.

THE TRIGGERS OF DESIRE

1. Childhood experiences

You are deeply affected by the first things you encounter. Your mind is like a blank slate waiting for life to write a story. Small children live every day with an explosion of neurological development. Their young minds continually examine and process their environment. For example, it has been fascinating to watch Levi, our grandson, discover the world. As of this writing, he is two years old and continually watches and learns. He experiments until he connects with the meaning of his activity. He soaks up stimulating input every minute. Levi is already forming his understanding of the world. Much of his exposure to everything from food to people is setting a standard that he will measure things by in the future. Because this process begins so early, his first experiences become part of the neurological network of his young brain. As he matures, these early inputs will create desires and interests that will surface at certain moments in his life. What is true of our grandson, is true of you. Your memory, both conscious and unconscious, continually provides images and emotions that move you toward certain things. That memory began to develop when you were a child.

The Big White House

I remember taking a walk with my mother when I was five years old. This memory is not completely clear, but I recall enough detail that I can still relive the comfortable feel of that spring day; the image of abundant flowers and trees, the security and joy that flowed from holding my mother's hand, and a mental picture of a big white house.

I am sure I had seen the white house before (it is a small town with a limited number of homes), but this was the first time I had noticed it. My mother stopped to speak with someone, and while she talked, I looked at the house, which stood on a corner lot near the edge of a fast-flowing mountain river. Hundreds of purple rhododendron blossoms framed an expansive front porch surrounded by tall columns, and a glass sunroom faced the riverside.

The house rose three stories above my head with a classic design filled with dozens of large windows. One window looked especially inviting to me, a dormer with wooden doors that extended from the front of the top story. To my young eyes, it seemed mysterious. I was curious to know what was behind it. We only stayed in front of the house for a few minutes. But it was long enough to form a lasting image in my mind. I decided that I wanted to live in that house someday, or at least one like it. I grew up, went to college and graduate school, married, had children, and launched my speaking career. We lived in a trailer, four apartments, and three houses, but I never lost my desire for the white house.

I am writing this book in the library of that house. Amy and I bought it 33 years after my five-year-old moment on the sidewalk. Your childhood experiences and memories are often clues to why you want what you want. They are the foundation of many of your desires.

2. Your first perceived heroes or mentors

Every child looks for an adult example to follow. Hopefully, the best adult examples are found in the child's parents. In the best circumstances, the father and mother provide the role model that guides the child.

But other role models exert influence. A teacher, coach, pastor, or relative, often impress positive qualities on a developing child. Even in the teen years, an adult may capture the attention of a young person and inspire better behavior and higher achievement.

A Surprise Question While Eating at a McDonalds Restaurant

I was having breakfast with my good friend, former congressman, Bob McEwan. We had both spoken at a conference and were having breakfast before leaving for the airport. Bob is a gifted speaker with an extensive network of famous and influential friends, and I asked him if he could recommend someone to help me analyze my methods and improve my skills. With no hesitation, he gave me the name of the man he said was the best at discerning the optimal direction for a company or an individual. Bob said the man served as a consultant for several widely known corporations. He warned me that the man charged $5000 per session but said he would ask him to meet with me as a favor to him (Bob).

Bob arranged the meeting, and Amy and I flew to Florida to spend time with a man I had never met. 1 arrived at a hotel he recommended, and we talked for an hour about our ministry goals. His insights were remarkable. He quickly uncovered problems and made valuable suggestions.

When we finished, I thought that I had received all I could hope for in a free session, but he said that he wanted to meet one more time. He told me that if I were willing, he could show me a crucial key to my future performance, but it would require a few hours of "homework" that night. He explained that the "homework" was necessary to help me understand "the key." I agreed, and he handed me a notebook with instructions and questions. He told me to study the assignments listed, answer the questions, and meet him the next morning at a McDonald's restaurant near the entrance to Walt Disney World.

I completed the assignments, rose early the next morning, had prayer, and went for a run. I arrived at the McDonalds found a table, and waited, filled with anticipation. The consultant entered the restaurant precisely on time, found me, and sat down. He greeted me and asked to see the questions I had answered the night before.

There were 100 questions, and it took time for him to scan my answers. When he finished, he asked me a surprising question. He wanted to know who my hero was when I was in fourth grade. I had not expected this question and had to quickly review my memories of fourth grade. At first, I was unable to arrive at an answer, but suddenly a face popped up in my mind. After a moment, I knew the answer to his question. I told the consultant that when I was ten years old (fourth grade), I was captivated by my Uncle Adrian, my mother's brother.

Adrian was a "bigger than life" character who filled every room he entered. He was immensely strong (my mother often told

the story of how he had saved her life as a child by physically stopping a car rolling down a hill by reaching his arm through an open window and pulling it to a stop). He was the successful owner of a multi-million-dollar company that drilled natural gas wells. He was loved by everyone who knew him because of his overflowing generosity. He once, during a downturn in his industry, gave up part of his salary to give his men bonuses (and turkeys for their families) at Christmas. He was impossible to intimidate, feared nothing but was also warm and kind. He lived to take care of other people.

I told the consultant what you just read and explained that, along with my father, who I loved and respected, I wanted to be like Uncle Adrian. That realization surfaced in the fourth grade. The consultant smiled and said that his years of research had revealed that young men and women often consciously find a hero to emulate at around ten years of age, in fourth grade. He had observed that this hero figure became a big part of the developing self-image of the young person.

The consultant then asked me to list some values that were important to me. I listed, generosity, fearlessness, advocacy, and protection for other people, financial independence based on ownership of your own business, and a happy, outgoing approach to life. He then asked me to list what I most admired about my Uncle Adrian. It was the same list.

He then explained that Uncle Adrian had not replaced my parents (who, as I said, I loved and respected) but had been the added hero image I had needed at that point in my young life. I was surprised to discover (with the help of the consultant) that my Uncle Adrian had guided my life without me even knowing it had happened.

I encourage you to do what I did that morning in Florida. Stop and identity people who have inspired you and guided your growth. Picture your first heroes. Recall how different individuals motivated you to improve. Remember your mentors. These individuals form parts of your self-image that you still carry.

3. Popular media images

Not all media images are positive. There are undoubtedly fictional characters in books and movies who are morally corrupt and irresponsible and whose example no one should follow, regardless of how "cool" they seem on the page or screen. Many young people have adopted bad and harmful habits because of the influence of a media personality who should have known better.

But there are good examples in media as well. I grew up with the popularity of Indiana Jones and Han Solo, characters who were brave and resourceful and always ended up on the side of good. As a boy, I was fascinated by Tarzan and John Carter of Mars, both created by legendary author Edgar Rice Burroughs. I wanted to be a fearless protector of those in need because

that is what these heroes did. When I discovered Sherlock Holmes, I
wanted to be as intelligent and observant as the great detective.
When I came into a relationship with Jesus Christ when I was thirteen, I
started to read the Bible. I discovered real historical figures like King David
of Israel and Elijah, the mighty prophet of God, who, unlike fictional
creations, gave examples of actual leadership that inspired me as a
teenager. These are not media figures from someone's imagination but
were still present through the "media" of the Bible. Some of the media
images that influence your desires are not of people at all. You may be
captivated by the scenery of another country in a film or decide you want to
visit a particular city that you just encountered in your reading. All these
images enter your mind and form ideas that pull you toward different
experiences. They all help create your desires.

4. Molding moments

A molding moment is a moment when something challenges your mind,
enters your heart, and changes your direction. It may be a comment in a
conversation, a picture on your phone, an insight delivered in a seminar, or
an encounter with someone new. Your experience becomes a "molding
moment" when that comment, picture, insight, or encounter awakens you to
a fresh possibility or provides an answer for which you were looking. It is a
"moment" that "molds" you in a way that leads you in a new direction, but
it only works when you ALLOW the "moment" to "mold" you.

The Preacher Who Never Preached

When I was a student at Asbury College (now Asbury University), I
attended a conference led by one of the most unusual men I have ever met.
He had left his church in Pennsylvania to move to New York City when he
saw a photograph in *Life Magazine* that startled him. It was a picture of

young gang members who were living lives devastated by drugs and violence.

David Wilkerson had no experience with gang culture but felt a wave of compassion for the young men and sensed that God wanted him to go to New York and spiritually help these gang members. He created a media sensation when he entered a courtroom where the young men in the picture were on trial. When Wilkerson interrupted the hearing and asked to speak to the young men, the judge ejected him from the courtroom. A reporter took Wilkerson's picture as he was escorted out, and a local newspaper published the photograph with a brief story. Suddenly Wilkerson was famous.

David Wilkerson stayed in the city and started a ministry to reach the youth gangs of New York. In 1958, he founded Teen Challenge, a Christian addiction recovery organization, and published a book about his adventures, *The Cross, and the Switchblade*, in 1963. The influential magazine *Christianity Today* listed the book in their list of the "Top 50 Books That Have Shaped Evangelicals". The book became an international bestseller and was made into a motion picture in 1970, starring Pat Boone as Wilkerson.

This was the man who was speaking at the conference on our campus. I was inspired by Wilkerson's passion and intrigued by his style of communication. He was a preacher who never "preached." He spoke in simple, clear, direct language and used words easy to understand. He was blunt and effective. He spoke as if he were sitting alone with you, telling you what you needed to hear. I had spent some time with him throughout the conference and decided to stay and speak with him following the final session.

I waited until everyone had left the auditorium and asked if I could talk with him. He agreed, and we sat down on the edge of the stage. I told him that I had never heard anyone speak like him and that the models I had followed to develop my speaking style all emphasized big words and flowery phrases. I was not sure that worked any longer and wanted his advice.

I then experienced a critical "molding moment." He asked me what I wanted to communicate, and I said I wanted to explain the reality of Jesus Christ and the power of Biblical principles to people who did not understand either. I wanted to help people find spiritual freedom. Wilkerson listened carefully then said that if I wanted to communicate the most important message in the world, then I had better make sure I explained everything in the most simple, direct way possible. He looked at me and said, "Ronnie, people don't need to hear from you. They need to hear God. You are just a "mouthpiece." Don't try to impress people with your fancy words. Just love them and tell them the truth as straightforwardly as you can. Say what you mean and mean what you say. Never leave any doubt about the meaning of your message."

When he finished, an image of him speaking flashed in my mind. I instantly saw what he meant. It was the way he spoke, in a way that was simple, clear, and direct. When he spoke, you understood what he had said. That one "molding moment" forever changed my approach to public communication. I may not always succeed, but, since that brief conversation, I have always tried to "get the message across." That "moment" taught me that the message is more important than the messenger.

Focus on your "molding moments." What did you learn? How did you change? How were you "molded"? Be alert to these opportunities for growth when they appear. They not only help mold your desires and dreams, but they may also be the unexpected signals that reveal what you should do and where you should go. They can increase your understanding of your ultimate purpose.

The list you just read reveals the sources of many of your desires and can help you understand why you want what you want. The list explains how many desires originate and why they appeal to you. But there are also desires that grow in your heart because they are specifically connected to the purpose you are meant to fulfill. These desires are rooted in your calling and a part of who you are. To discover and complete your mission, you need to uncover these deeper desires as well.

The Clarity Test

Here is a list of questions that can help you clarify the desires that express who you really are. When you honestly answer each question, those answers can become a map that leads to your mission.

1. What do you think about most of the time?

My friend and mentor, Charles Stanley, would often ask me one question when we met to talk and plan. He usually opened our time by asking, "Well, Ron, what have you been thinking about today?" He once explained to me that he always led with that question because he had found that you think about what you care about. Your thoughts reveal your deepest interests and motivations. Take a moment and focus on what has most occupied your thoughts today. If you think mostly about bills, debts, and financial obligations, then you probably need to form a plan to achieve financial independence. If you mostly think about your family, then that should strengthen your commitment to improving your relationships. Your thoughts are a window into your priorities. You should carefully analyze what you think about to determine what you care about.

2. What do you watch?

We live in a media drenched world. Personal time is filled with screen time. Research has discovered that when you allow something into your mind, your brain perceives it as real. That is why you become so emotionally involved in a movie or television show. As you watch the images on the screen, your brain accepts the reality of what you see. It is easy to absorb messages from the stories you watch whether you want to or not.

Because of this, you need to discipline yourself. You may see a show as entertainment, but layers of hidden communication still influence you. Screenwriters and movie directors know that when they create a scene with likable, engaging characters with exciting action and visual stimulation, they can easily plant an idea or impression within that scene.

This is especially true of humor. Brain research has found that humor temporarily blocks the activity of the pre-frontal cortex, the part of your brain that makes rational decisions. When you are laughing, you are not thinking.

Early movie makers were careful not to present an immoral or deceptive character in an attractive manner. They did not want to create a negative and harmful role model for people (especially young people). This does not mean that all entertainment is filled with dangerous, secret messages. But because some of it is, you need to intelligently filter what you watch, whether on a big screen in a theater, a private screen in your home, or the portable screen in your pocket. What you allow into your mind does have influence.

What you watch is also connected to your life goals. There is nothing wrong with wanting to engage with a movie or program to relax or learn something new. There are times when you want to see a film or watch a show or podcast because you are interested in the content. You also, at times, just want to watch something you think is fun. But always be alert to what your viewing schedule reveals about you. What you choose to enjoy reveals what you believe is moral or good. Your viewing habits are another window into yourself.

Because media is so powerful, I recommend that you concentrate on programs that encourage you, strengthen your positive attitude, feed you useful information, and help you become the person you want to be. Use the media in your life to become a better person so you can advance your mission and fulfill your purpose.

3. What do you talk about?

Take a day and monitor your conversation. What can you learn about yourself by what you choose to talk about?

The Hidden Bible Study Agenda

My wife attended a Bible study group when we lived in Atlanta, Georgia. The group was popular with couples our age, and we enjoyed the interactions. The study was led by a sincere, older man who worked hard to deliverer practical and helpful information from different books of the Bible (66 different books make up the Bible).

The group followed the same format every time. We mingled and talked for about fifteen minutes to reconnect with one another; then, when we sat down, the study leader asked if anyone had a particular need or concern that we could pray for. One woman always responded first. She would express concern for an individual then ask us to pray for that person, and when she finished, she always added the person's name and gave details about their situation, often including something they had done wrong. She ended by saying that she only provided the additional information because she wanted us to pray for them.

One evening the meeting began as usual, and when we sat for the study, the woman, as she always did, offered the first prayer request, but this time she asked for prayer for a couple we all knew. After she mentioned their names, she said that she wanted us to know why we were praying for the couple. Then she said (I still remember it): "Have you heard what is going on in their marriage? A friend told me that David is having an affair, and Rachel just found out. We need to pray for them." An uncomfortable silence descended on the room. Suddenly I realized what was wrong. This woman was not sharing prayer requests; she was using the group time as an opportunity to spread harmful gossip. She may or may not have cared about the people she mentioned, but she loved broadcasting dirt on other people. When the meeting ended, I spoke with the Bible study leader about the woman. He told me that he had also noticed her misuse of the meeting and believed that she attended to advance her agenda. He added that several other people had expressed the same concern. He promised to speak with her. He did, and she never returned.

The Bible says in Ephesians 4:29, "Do *not let any unwholesome talk come out of your mouths, but only what is helpful for building others up according to their needs, that it may benefit those who listen."* The woman at the Bible study injured people by her words as she invaded their privacy and exposed their needs. Her priority should have been to "build them up" and spiritually support them.

Listen to yourself. Are you positive or negative? Helpful or harmful? Encouraging or discouraging? Self-centered or focused on others? Critical or healing? Do you ask questions that help you grow or push your opinions? Do you show respect for the views of other people or respond with criticism and judgment? What you say and how you say it can be a signpost that tells you if you are on the right road.

4. Who do you listen to?

The Brother's Bad Advice

There are people you casually listen to who have little influence on you because you pay little attention to them and what they say There are other people who you listen to because you respect them and want to follow their example. These people have enormous influence over you.

I once visited my friend Dexter Yager, who led a large Amway organization. When I arrived at his home on Lake Wylie in South Carolina, another couple was finishing a session with Dexter, and I waited on a deck overlooking a wide bend in the lake. After a few minutes, Dexter came to the door and asked me into the room. I entered and saw that the couple was still present. Dexter told me that the couple (whom I knew) had agreed to include me in their discussion. I sat on a soft sofa and listened to their story. The couple had developed a significant business and had decided to invest part of their profits. The husband had a background in college athletics and still participated in sports competitions. He explained that his older brother had come to him with an investment idea, but when he and his wife examined the opportunity, they thought it presented too much risk and too little return.

They decided to reject the investment, but the husband s brother asked them to reconsider. The man telling me the story explained that he loved his older brother and had always wanted to be like him as they grew up together. His brother was the better athlete and had ridden his abilities to popularity and success in school. Unfortunately, that success ended with high school. The older brother failed to finish college (where he had won an athletic scholarship) and had experienced a series of business failures through his early and middle adult years. When his little brother shared the Amway opportunity with him, he laughed at their "foolishness" and told them they were making a "big mistake." Even when the younger brother and his wife reached a high level of success with their Amway opportunity, he still treated their business with contempt.

Despite this adverse history, when the older brother asked that the couple reconsider their rejection of his idea, the younger brother changed his position and decided to invest. The wife still objected, and that had brought them to Dexter for counsel and direction.

When the man concluded his story, Dexter asked if anyone had noticed what was wrong with his account. No one answered. Dexter repeated the question, and a flicker of realization struck my mind. I told the couple that I meant no disrespect to them or their business judgment but that I had one question. I asked them why, with the brothers bad 'track record", they would take business advice from him. I added that it did not seem that he had earned the right to counsel them.

Dexter said that was precisely the point he wanted to make. He just wanted it to come from someone other than him to reinforce the insight. The couple looked embarrassed, and, after a moment, the wife turned to her husband and reassured him of her love and support. She paused and asked him what he thought of my comment. The husband replied that he was worried about the investment but struggled with the love he felt for his brother. He said he knew he had made a wrong decision and was sorry for the stress he had caused his wife. He promised to cancel the investment and asked us to pray for his brother. His wife smiled with relief.

After the couple left, Dexter asked me what I thought was the lesson to learn from the conversation. I said that you should always be careful who you listen to. Dexter laughed and said that it still surprised him how often people took business advice from people who were not successful in business. He then said, "why would a person who needs money seek counsel from a person who is broke?" He finished with a reminder that you should follow the example of people who live the life you hope to live. Do not follow people who violate your beliefs and do not understand your mission. If you care about your purpose, you will avoid input from people who do not support your vision. You should only seek guidance from individuals who care about you and believe in your purpose. These are the people who you can depend on to protect your dream. These are the people you can trust. These are the people you should listen to.

5. Who do you spend time with?

Most people think of investment in terms of money, but how you invest your time is even more important. How you choose to spend your time determines your opportunities. You may not have as much money as someone else, but you have the same amount of time as everyone else. I understand that certain blocks of your time are committed to different responsibilities, but you still have many hours every week you can give to your life-purpose. How you choose to use those hours can determine your happiness and fulfillment in life. You decide what to do with your free time and you decide who to spend time with. Make wise choices.

The Frustrated Woman

I was friends in college with a young woman from my hometown. She was a sweet, uncomplicated person who delighted to help people. She made friends easily, and everyone liked her. One afternoon she told me that a young man had asked her for a date, and she was deciding if she should say yes. She was a deeply committed Christian and hoped for a successful Christian marriage, but the young man had no interest in the Christian faith. He had bad habits she disagreed with, but she believed that her influence would improve him.

This young woman decided to date the young man, and in less than six months, she was in a tornado of distress and disappointment. To please him, she agreed to stop going to church. Soon the spiritual commitment that had meant so much to her began to weaken. She experimented with drugs to "be close to him" and moved into sexual areas that she had previously determined to avoid.

When I saw her at a restaurant in our hometown, she was depressed and distant. Her joy and vitality were gone. When I asked her about her plans, she said that she had decided to leave college and move to another town to be with her "boyfriend." I asked what his plans were, and she said that he was looking for work and hoped to find something soon.

Thankfully, this story has a happy ending. My friend awoke to the danger of her situation, left her boyfriend, renewed her relationship with Christ, and returned to college. She eventually met and married a young man who shared her spiritual commitment. He became a successful medical doctor.

She, her husband, and four children have been happy and productive for many years.

The lesson here is that, although you may think you have the inner strength to hold to your values, the people you choose to associate with create a powerful pull in their direction. Imagine standing on a chair and locking hands with someone standing on the floor in front of you. You are larger and heavier than the individual on the floor, but when you both pull against one another, the person on the floor will always pull you down because the force of gravity increases their power. They will win every time. This is why an individual with bad habits, or a negative attitude is such a danger to your progress. The "gravity" of their influence pulls you down from your best intentions and makes it difficult to be who you want to be. This is what happened to my friend, and it required a great effort for her to free herself from the harmful influence of her boyfriend. Be careful who you spend time with, that choice alone is a critical factor in your success or failure.

6. What angers you?

I am not referring here to selfish anger where you react because you do not get what you want. This is a different form of anger that rises within you because you encounter something wrong or unfair. What makes you angry you can reveal what you care about.

The Television Confrontation

When I was thirteen years old (and a new Christian), I was watching a television documentary with my parents. The program featured reporting on child abuse around the world. As I watched the graphic scenes of innocent children starved and beaten, I suddenly stood up and waved my fist at the TV screen. Anger flared up in my spirit and overflowed into our living room. My parents looked surprised and asked me what was wrong. I was embarrassed for a moment then explained that I was angry over the mistreatment of the children. This experience revealed that I cared deeply about injustice (and still do).

Many years later, when our daughter Allison was the assistant county attorney in our home county in Kentucky, she was responsible for prosecuting child abuse cases. She shared my "good anger" at individuals who abused children and worked to protect as many children as possible. I was immensely proud of her commitment to justice. It connected with my distaste for unfairness in any form. Be alert to what creates an angry response in you. The source of your anger probably represents a cause that you should support or a wrong you should help to make right. There may be a clue to your purpose in your reaction.

7. What "needs" touch your heart?

The world is filled with human needs. You cannot meet them all, but there are always specific needs that especially reach your heart. These are the needs that will not leave you alone. You sense a desire to help and cannot escape the sense that you need to act on that need. When this happens, it may be a clue to the definition of your purpose. Your purpose is often connected to those needs that capture your attention. Part of your mission may be to help meet those needs.

The Rejected Wife

Amy and I were speaking at a conference in south Alabama. Following a morning session, we were invited by a woman to join her for lunch at her country club. She was a slim, attractive woman in her late forties, blessed with a vivacious personality. We liked her immediately.

We sat at a table overlooking a beautifully groomed golf course. It was a quiet, easy atmosphere with servers dressed in white, moving efficiently among the tables. When we finished the meal, the woman asked if we would pray for her. She said that her husband, the owner of a construction company, had told her he wanted a divorce. He said he had "fallen in love" with a young woman he had met while on a project and wanted to continue his life with her.

The woman expressed shock and pain as she described her situation. Her two children were young adults who had left home, graduated from college, and were now building lives and careers of their own. She said that she had always loved her husband and had been anticipating many more happy years together. She was baffled by this new development and uncertain of what to do. She needed help. Amy and I responded with concern and compassion.

We assured her of God's love and promised to pray for her. We completed our time together and left to prepare for the next session of the conference. Later that night, I remembered our conversation. I had been deeply affected by the woman and her personal tragedy.

I grew up in a home where my parents loved and supported one another (they recently celebrated their 70th wedding anniversary) and was happily married to Amy (and still am). The happiness I had experienced made me want everyone to share the same marital joy. The need the woman expressed at lunch created in me a strong desire to help her. The next day Amy and I contacted her and offered our continued support.

Twenty years later, I was asked by the owner of a company I had spoken for if I had any information that could improve the marriages of his top executives. He shared his concern that marriage challenges were compromising the performance of his leaders, and he asked if I could help. I immediately had the same response I had felt twenty years earlier after the conversation with the rejected wife at the country club. I told the owner that I would create a program for his executives. I was motivated by a desire to save other wives from the bitter experience of the woman who had touched my heart years before. I wanted to help men be happy husbands who protected and cared for their wives and children and nourished and sustained their families.

Six months later, I presented a seminar on successful marriage to the top-level executives of the company and gave them a program to enhance their relationships and resolve problems. The response was enormous. The program was so productive that the company owner contacted owners of other companies and recommended they use my seminar as well.

This success led to the development of a new addition to my speaking schedule. Amy and I created a weekend opportunity we named Honeymoon for Life, that we added to the leadership seminars we already offered. We developed a weekend that blended fun and information. We organized the event to especially appeal to men so they would want to attend with their wives because we had noticed that men often were reluctant to participate in marriage enrichment opportunities.

The results were far beyond our expectations. To date, over 11,000 couples have attended these Honeymoon for Life conferences, and 90% of attendees return for repeat weekends. God has significantly blessed this outreach. Our response to the needs of a woman in Alabama led us to an understanding that marriage enrichment is part of our mission. Our desire to meet a need brought us to a pathway into our purpose.

CHAPTER 8
How to Avoid Purpose Blockage

Amy and I were driving from Charlotte, North Carolina, to Knoxville, Tennessee, one September morning. We were traveling on Interstate 40 and planning to stop in Gatlinburg, Tennessee for lunch. As we entered the curvy stretch of the interstate that crossed through the Pisgah National Forest, we were stopped by road barriers and warning signs. The signs told us that a landslide had closed the interstate requiring us to detour through Cherokee, North Carolina, and into the Great Smoky Mountains National Park.

We arrived at our destination hours behind schedule. There are times when your life purpose encounters unexpected blockages and detours. You may find yourself off your planned path and traveling through unknown territory. What do you do?

Your Four Choices

When you realize that you have lost your way and your mission is missing, you have four simple choices.

1. **First,** you can surrender. You can retire your dream and accept your new limited life. You can join the great, mediocre middle mass of people who are neither hot nor cold. You will still feel the pain of your loss but can manage your stress by self-medication through alcohol and drugs or hide from your unhappiness through excessive entertainment or uncontrolled sexuality. You can numb yourself by surrendering to boring routines that steal your time and leave you unsatisfied. You can "give up."

2. **Second,** you can struggle. You can substitute a lesser goal for your true purpose. You can throw yourself into projects that do good but keep you from the best. You can fight just enough to ease your guilt and lower your pain but never breakthrough to the summit of your purpose. You can choose to pursue a pale, weak version of your purpose so you will not need to pay the price to accomplish your true-life goals. You will struggle because you want to fulfill your purpose but do not give the commitment to "go all the way."

3. **Third,** you can stretch and grow and use your time on the detour to clarify your direction and learn lessons that will prepare you for greater success. You can expand your skills and deepen your mind. You can throw out unnecessary baggage that slows you down. You can use the detour to become better, smarter, wiser, and stronger. You can learn how to find the entrance ramp back onto the highway of your purpose.

4. **Fourth,** you can soar. A detour is an opportunity to develop an awesome positive attitude. Blockages and detours reveal who you are. Delays and difficulties are a graduate course in success. Learn to not focus on the length of the detour, but to focus on getting back on the path. Decide to stop the surrender and cease the struggle caused by half-heartedness. Decide to stretch and soar. When you do this, then you are ready to confront and overcome the blockages in your way.

The Blockages

Here is a list of many of the blockages you may encounter on your "purpose highway."

1. Insufficient Funds

The Credit Card Embarrassment

My first credit card was a Sears card. I was a student with a $500 credit limit and no awareness of how to manage money or credit. I charged several items over the first two weeks then returned to the store on a Saturday to continue shopping. I found several things I thought I needed and carried them to a pay station. I had not tracked my purchases and was unprepared when the woman checking me out told me that my card had been declined.

There were five people in line behind me, and each one stared at me. I mumbled an apology in my embarrassment, placed the items on the counter, and left. It was my first experience with "insufficient funds." But when I refer to "insufficient funds" in this book, I am not writing about money, I am writing about the inner resources you need to find and fulfill your purpose. Sometimes God allows a detour because you need more preparation and deeper maturity to complete your purpose. You do not have "sufficient funds" within yourself, and until you do, you are not ready to complete your purpose.

From Prison to Prime Minister

Many years ago, Amy and I attended a conference on ministry methods used to attract teenagers to the Christian faith. The auditorium was jammed with eager attendees, and the information was fresh, original, and usable. After the final session, the speaker gave a warning. He said that after God reveals a vision for your life, you often pass through a phase he called 'the death of the vision." It is while you are traveling through this valley that you learn the lessons you need to move forward. The speaker then added that when those lessons are learned, you exit the valley, and the vision returns.

This was the experience of a young man who was the favorite child of his aging father. His father lavished so many gifts on him that his brothers became jealous. The young man made the situation worse when he told his father and brothers that God had given him a vision of the future where they were all subordinate to him. The young man's vision disappointed his father and enraged his brothers.

One morning the young man's father sent him to check on a project his brothers were engaged in and return with a report. The young man found his brothers, but instead of welcoming their younger brother, they decided to murder him. They were preparing to kill him when the oldest brother intervened and persuaded the brothers to toss the young man into a well and leave him to die. The elder brother was secretly planning to rescue his brother later. The plans changed when a caravan of slavers arrived. The brothers then decided to sell their brother into slavery and tell their father a wild animal had killed him.

In just a few hours, the privileged and pampered life of this young man was destroyed. He was carried to the capital of the superpower of the time and sold to a prominent official.

Through a series of strange and dramatic events, he lost his position in the service of the official and was put in prison. He was seventeen years old. The young man had lost his freedom, his dignity, and his future. In the damp darkness of the prison, he must have remembered the vision of success and authority God had shown him only months before. It must have seemed more a nightmare than a vision. Doubts tore at his soul, and he must have thought that God had abandoned him. He could not imagine a way out.

This young man was experiencing "the death of a vision," but while he was in his "valley of death," his relationship with God deepened. He learned to adapt to his circumstances and offered to help the men who managed the prison. For the next year, he developed such effective leadership and management skills that the warden put him in charge of the prison.

A crisis in the government caused two high ranking officials to be sent to the same prison. The young man befriended both men and months after the release of one of the men, another crisis threatened the government. The king asked his advisors for direction, and when none of them could answer his questions, the man who had been in prison remembered the extraordinary young man he had met while imprisoned. He told the king that the young man had a gift for interpreting events and suggested that the king bring him from the prison to the palace for a consultation.

When the young man arrived, the king told him of a disturbing and mysterious dream he had had repeatedly. The dream pictured plants that ate other plants and cows that ate other cows. The king said he had been told that the young man had a gift for explaining dreams and that he expected an answer. The young man had learned humility in prison and immediately told the king that he could interpret the dream, but the answer would come from God and not from his personal abilities.

He then told the king the meaning of the dream. A severe famine was coming, and God had given a warning in the dream. The only hope for survival was an extensive and well-organized system of crop management and food storage. The young man urged the king to find a man with the required skills and place him in charge of the life-saving project.

The king then surprised everyone when he told those assembled that the right man was in the room. He gave the young man authority over the entire country, second only to himself, and told him to organize and lead the nation through the coming crisis. In one dramatic moment, the young man had gone from prison to the position of Prime Minister of the country. The famine came as the young man had predicted, but he had already instituted a remarkable plan that guaranteed plenty of food for everyone. As the famine worsened, leaders from other regions contacted the more prominent nation for help.

One day a group of men arrived with money to buy grain and were presented to the Prime Minister. In an emotionally ripping meeting, the Prime Minister realized the delegation who had come to buy grain were the brothers who had sold him into slavery.

They bowed to him just as he had seen in the vision when he was seventeen. He hid his knowledge of their identity and sold them grain but planted a valuable gold cup in their luggage. He then sent a servant to intercept the group, pulled the "stolen" cup from the bags and ordered the men to return. He kept one brother as a hostage to guarantee their return and sent them home.

A series of events led to a banquet where the young man revealed his identity, which eventually led to a joyous reunion with his father, who also bowed to his authority as Prime Minister, fulfilling the rest of the vision. The brothers, the father, and all their family members moved to the country where the young man ruled. Their lives were saved, and the young man's purpose was fulfilled. The story of Joseph described in the book of Genesis, chapters 37-50, is a powerful historical account of a young man who received a vision of his purpose, lost his vision, then recovered his purpose. He passed from the youthful excitement of his purpose through the valley of loss and death and into the sunlight of the rebirth of his vision.

When their father died, the brothers were afraid that Joseph would take revenge on them, but Joseph had matured through his experiences into a gracious and Godly leader. He demonstrated that he understood his mission when he told the brothers, *"Don't be afraid. Am I in the place of God? You intended to harm me, but God intended it for good to accomplish what is now being done, the saving of many lives."* (Genesis 50:19-21 NIV)

When Joseph received his original vision at seventeen, he did not have the maturity, knowledge, or skills to fulfill his purpose. He had INSUFFICIENT FUNDS.

God took him through several years of training and development to prepare him for authority and responsibility and "the saving of many lives" When he became Prime Minister of Egypt, his inner account was "fully funded."

2. Bog Wallowing

Monsters at Midnight

I have told the story of my childhood weekends with my grandmother Ball in my book, *Dynamic Leadership Skills*. If you have read that book, you may recall the late-night monster movies we watched together. It was a special treat for me to eat freshly baked gingerbread (a specialty of my grandmother), and endless bowls of popcorn.

But the best thing about the evening was the old black and white monster movies we watched on Chiller Theater until midnight on Saturday night. These films, of course, were mild compared to later movies. There was no blood and gore and no graphic violence. The monsters were always defeated, and good always won. When we finished, I went right to bed so I could be up early the next morning for Sunday School and church.

When I look back on those films now, I am surprised how many contained scenes that took place in swamps or bogs filled with quicksand and confusing vegetation. Often a person, fleeing the monster, would stumble over vines and rocks and end up stuck in a bog, unable to move. They were trapped.

This is what happens when you become confused about your direction and become stuck in a bog of mistakes and dead ends. Instead of fighting your way out of the bog, you collapse into defeat and discouragement. The longer you wallow in the bog, the harder it is to get out.

The Couple on the Beach

Several years ago, Amy and I and our family were on vacation at Walt Disney World in Florida. We were staying in Ft. Wilderness campground in an RV trailer and every evening Amy, and I walked on the beach of Bay Lake.

On the first night, we met a couple who had lived near our former home in Georgia. We liked one another and enjoyed a natural conversation. We walked with this couple every night for the rest of the week and became comfortable with one another's company.

One evening, after our walk, I returned to the beach and encountered the husband standing near a boat dock. He seemed down, and I asked him if he was concerned about something. He told me that he and his wife had had an argument and he was on the beach to think and reflect on what she had said. Without my asking, he then told me that they had had the same argument many times. He felt stuck in a continual cycle of the same words and thoughts. I asked him what the argument was about, and he said that he had a bad habit of discussing a problem for weeks without arriving at a resolution. His wife was frustrated with the seemingly endless conversations and had become worn down by the constant repetition. The husband admitted that he had the same conversation every night and did say the same things again and again. Even worse, the more he repeated the conversation, the more negative and critical he became.

I asked him if he was familiar with the psychological concept of rumination. I had studied this condition in graduate school, and his description seemed to fit this type of response. When he said that he was unfamiliar with the word, I explained that rumination is an obsessive review of negative thoughts that can dominate a person's mind. The Merriam-Webster dictionary defines rumination as "a focusing of one's attention on negative or distressing thoughts or feelings that when excessive or prolonged may lead to or exacerbate an episode of depression."

When I finished my explanation, he seemed relieved. He smiled and said that I had accurately described what he had been doing. He understood the process I had explained and was eager to change. He realized that he had developed a habit of rehashing negative and stressful experiences and that he had pulled his wife into that same negative orbit. He thanked me and hurried away to see his wife.

This man was wallowing in a bog of negativity and confusion. The bog had become his world, and he needed a way out. This is what happens when you splash into a bog or a swamp while following your purpose. When you allow yourself to wallow in disturbing doubts and nagging negatives, you distract yourself from your purpose.

The Positive Pastor

When I was in college, I had a class where I was required to sample different speeches from numerous people in leadership positions. I read the text of speeches by political figures, media personalities, and famous writers.

After I had finished 2/3 of the reading, I came to a sermon that had been delivered over twenty-five years before by an influential pastor of a large metropolitan church in New York City. The message was interesting and well-prepared, and I was enjoying the content when I came to a section that especially inspired me. The pastor paused in his presentation and addressed his listeners directly and forcefully. He said that there was no good reason for a Christian to live a life of negativity and doubt. Of all people in the world, Christians had the most solid foundation for living with optimism and excitement. He then added that he realized that it is common to have doubts but that, instead of being defeated by doubt, you should "doubt your doubts" and "believe your beliefs."

This was my first introduction to the importance of maintaining a vigorous positive attitude. I was so touched that I found a recording of the pastor's message so I could listen to it as he delivered it. When the recording came to the section where the pastor spoke about doubt and belief, his voice became more intense and dynamic energy throbbed from his vocal cords as he pushed the words out. When he said, "doubt your doubts and believe your beliefs," the power in his words swept over me. I knew that this man believed what he was saying.

This is the opposite of "wallowing" in a bog of negativity and fear. There will be moments when you doubt your purpose and think yourself mistaken in your mission, but if you are certain that you are on the right track, then you should "doubt your doubts and believe your beliefs," pull yourself from the swamp and move forward toward your destiny. Mental "bog wallowing" will only make you sink into a life of disappointment and disillusionment. Your most significant battlefield is your mind. The Bible says in Romans 12:2, "Do *not conform to the pattern of this world but be transformed by the renewing of your mind!"* NIV. This verse is a reminder that your battles are won or lost in the privacy of your thoughts. Philippians 4:8 says, *"finally, brothers and sisters, whatever is true, whatever is noble, whatever is right,*

-

whatever is pure, whatever is lovely, whatever is admirable-if anything is excellent or praiseworthy-think about such things."

You can choose your thoughts. You are not at the mercy of your mind. Recent research on the brain has determined that the thoughts you think create their own emotional response. This is known as the "thought sequence," and this is how it works.

First, you think a thought; then the thought causes the transmission of an electrical signal. The electrical signal causes a chemical to be released, and the chemical creates an emotional response that matches the original thought. The emotion does not create the thought; the thought creates the emotion. Research has confirmed that it is your thoughts, positive or negative, that cause your feelings.

Even the chemical released by the electrical charge, triggered by your thought, is "shaped" by the thought. Positive thoughts lead to positively shaped "chemical keys," and negative thoughts produce negatively shaped "chemical keys." This is why "bog wallowing" is so dangerous.

But if you fall into a mental "bog," how do you get out? The answer is in your mind. Your doubts and negative thoughts put you in the bog, and your thoughts can get you out. One of the critical keys to success and prosperity is mental discipline. Many people are controlled by their emotions, but you can control your emotions by what you choose to think. If you dwell on fear, doubt, and worry (rumination), then you will create emotions of fear, doubt, and worry. If you focus on optimism, belief, positive expectation, and confidence, then you will produce emotions that support those happy thoughts. You can escape the bog through the pathways of your mind. This is especially important when you face challenges and difficulties. Every path has boulders and cracks that require you to climb over or go around if you want to reach your destination. At those times, discouragement is your greatest enemy. To punch through the barriers, you must discipline your thoughts and not allow yourself to surrender to defeatism.

Crying on the Stairs

One year after Amy and I incorporated The Ron Ball Association to organize our ministry, we hired a man to manage our new company. We had known him for several years and appreciated his reputation for efficiency and competence. We were excited to have him on the team. We left him in charge of all operations while we traveled and conducted conferences and seminars.

Six months after we hired him, we did a two-week speaking tour and then returned home for a short break. I opened the door to our apartment, turned on the lights, and retrieved the mail for the previous two weeks. I carried the mail to the kitchen, spread it on a table, and sat down to sort the items. The third envelope was from the IRS. I opened it, read the enclosed letter, and dropped it in shock. It was a notice that our payroll taxes had not been paid and that if the taxes and penalties were not paid by the next week, criminal charges would be filed against me. The amount was $8270.18.

We were in the early stages of our ministry outreach and made little money. All this happened before the Internet, so I called an automated phone service used by our bank to check on our balance. My sense of shock and dismay only increased when the computer voice reported my balance was overdrawn.

Amy was upstairs unpacking and knew nothing of what had just happened. When she finished, she found me sitting on the stairs, crying. Horrible, frightening thoughts flooded my mind. I remember thinking that our life and ministry were over. Gloom and despair descended on me. Amy sat beside me and asked what was wrong. I told her, and she just sat quietly with her hand on my shoulder. Then something wonderful happened. I remembered God's promises of provision and protection that I had memorized from the Bible. My favorite verse, Isaiah 41:10, burst into my mind, *"So do not fear, for I am with you; do not be dismayed, for I am your God. I will strengthen you and help you; I will uphold you with my righteous right hand"*.

I immediately shifted my attention from the scary thoughts that had been swirling through my mind and replaced them with the statement from God's word. Instantly my emotions calmed, and clarity and peace took over. I shared the verse with Amy, and we prayed for God to provide what we needed.

That night as I prepared to sleep, every time negative, fearful thoughts invaded my mind. I mentally quoted the verse and intentionally thanked God for keeping His promises. I slept well.

The next morning (Monday), I called our bank and discovered that our manager had withdrawn all our money. I next found that he had disappeared and was unreachable. Not only had he taken the money, but he had also not paid our taxes or filed the required legal forms. We never recovered the money and never saw him again. However, none of this knowledge solved our problem with the IRS.

For the rest of the day, we struggled unsuccessfully to find the money. It appeared hopeless, but we were determined not to return to the mental bog that had threatened to suck us down. We continued to pray, focus on positive, Bible-based thoughts, and trust God. The day ended with no change in our circumstances.

The next morning, I was in our kitchen when I suddenly felt that I should call a woman in my hometown who was a friend of my parents. I only knew her casually. I searched for and found her name and called. When she answered, I told her that I was calling because we were in a crisis, and we needed people to pray for us. She asked what was wrong, and I poured out the entire story in a

few minutes. When I stopped, she asked me how much money we needed, and I gave her the exact amount. She then quietly said, "I have your money." I thought she had misunderstood and repeated my prayer request, but she simply repeated, "I have your money."

She then explained that she used a giving account to donate money to different Christian ministries. She had planned to send all the funds in the account to a large, nationally recognized ministry organization but had felt the day before (Monday) that she should wait because the money was for someone who would call for it on Tuesday (the day I was calling). She then dropped an emotional bomb into our conversation. She told me that the exact amount in her giving account was $8270.18.

I was so overcome that I could not speak for a moment. I thanked her (and God) and gave her an address for the check. It arrived on Thursday. The IRS deadline was Friday. God had miraculously provided for us. If I had stayed in the mental bog of doubt, fear, and confusion, I would probably not have called the woman. Remember, the bog is not your friend.

3. Trivial Pursuit

There are many exciting and enjoyable things in life. It is not wrong to relax and appreciate a good meal or a beautiful scene. It is not wrong to play a game or watch a sporting event. But when you let yourself be distracted away from your purpose those things can create roadblocks on your way. When your attention is diverted away from your mission, you are experiencing "trivial pursuit."

The House Lost by Tennis

Amy and I were visiting friends in Atlanta, Georgia. We met at a downtown hotel and spent the evening together. The husband was rising in his company but had accumulated too much debt. His wife had aggravated their situation by charging every credit card to the max.

They had decided to spend the night at the hotel, and we were walking them to their room when the wife started to cry. We stopped and politely waited. When she finished, she apologized and said that their house mortgage payments were five months late, and they were about to lose their home.

We knew the couple well and I asked if anything could save their home. The husband said that he had an opportunity to make more money at another job but did not want to accept it. I asked if the new position involved a move and he said that it was in the same city where they lived. I then asked why, considering their desperate financial situation, he had declined the offer. I did not expect his answer. He said that he loved playing tennis, and the new job would not allow him the extra time to play tennis on Thursday nights. His wife started to cry again.

This man was engaged in "trivial pursuit" There is nothing wrong with tennis, but there is everything wrong with making tennis more important than caring for your family. He continued to play tennis on Thursday nights, and they lost their home and their marriage. When you transfer your time and energy to things that are not important and sacrifice your big dream for "fillers," you are playing "trivial pursuit." Many things are good, but they become "trivial" when compared to the greatness of your purpose. In the example of the man who lost his home because of his obsessive love of tennis, he had abandoned his purpose to care for and protect his family. He traded what mattered for the trivial.

4. Excuse Momentum

In my high school science classes, I learned about **inertia.** Inertia was originally defined by the greatest scientist of all time, Isaac Newton, who noted that an object that is standing still will remain in its position until some more powerful force makes it
move. If an object is already moving, it takes a more powerful force to stop it. This means that it is easier to stay in one place if you are not moving and easier to keep moving if you are already traveling forward.

When you stop growing and cease trying to advance, you will experience "purpose inertia." The longer you remain where you are, the harder it is to start moving again. You are stuck. Because you want to believe good things about yourself, you will often make excuses that seem reasonable but only cover up your failure to move forward. These excuses create their own "excuse momentum." The more you use them, the easier it is to believe them.

Some common excuses are:

- I am too old. I have missed my opportunity.

- I am too young. I do not have the experience I need.

- I do not know enough.

- I do not have enough money.

- I do not have enough help.

- I do not have enough education.

- Everything is too hard.

You can, of course, expand this list of excuses, but this sample reveals the true nature of an excuse. An excuse is a technique you use when you do not want to pursue your purpose. An excuse is a negative seed planted in the soil of your dream that eventually sprouts, spreads, and takes over.

The Invasion of The Vine

When I was nineteen years old, I was selected as a speaker on a team sponsored by my college. Four of us were selected, me, another speaker, and two singer-musicians. The school arranged an extensive summer schedule of events that took us through the southern United States, across Texas, and into Pennsylvania. It was a spectacular experience. We conducted meetings in churches, public auditoriums, and open-air arenas, and with excellent attendance in every location. We held rallies in small towns, worked for two weeks with Hispanic churches in the Rio Grande region of Texas, led a multi-church, city-wide crusade at the Monroe, Louisiana civic center, and held services at the largest church in the Christian and Missionary Alliance denomination in Pittsburgh, Pennsylvania. We ended the summer with a county-wide crusade in McCreary County, Kentucky.
At nineteen, I had rarely traveled outside my home state of Kentucky, and I was dazzled by the sights and scenes I encountered.
I still remember driving through Mississippi early one morning. We had traveled all night to fulfill a commitment in Louisiana and were moving through Mississippi as the summer sun rose behind us. It was my turn to drive while the other members of the team slept. As the sun cut through the morning mist, I saw that the interstate was lined on both sides by lush, deep green vegetation. It seemed that we were traveling through an exuberant jungle. I thought the plants were beautiful.
Later, after arriving at our hotel in Louisiana, we went to a restaurant to eat dinner. I began a conversation with a farmer and his wife at the next table and mentioned the

unusual plant cover I had seen on the drive. He laughed and said that what I had seen was not a friendly plant. It was kudzu, and everyone hated it because it so dominated every area it touched. He called it "the invader vine." He admitted that it was interesting to look at, but the vine's super-fast rate of growth made it almost impossible to control. It quickly smothered everything in its path.

I later discovered that kudzu is not native to North America. The name is Japanese, and it originated in Southeast Asia. It was introduced to the United States at the Japanese pavilion at the 1876 Centennial Exposition in Philadelphia. The exposition was a "world's fair" organized to celebrate the 100th anniversary of the Declaration of Independence and the founding of the American republic.

In the 1930s, conservation workers spread kudzu as a ground cover to prevent soil erosion, but no one anticipated its explosive growth. Under favorable conditions, kudzu can expand over 150,000 acres per year. Soon it covered many areas of the southern United States where hot, wet summer weather was like conditions in its native Asia. Excuses are the "kudzu" that threatens to stop your progress and smother your purpose. Like kudzu, "excuse momentum" expands rapidly until your excuses dominate your life. As kudzu replaces the vegetation it covers, your excuses replace your dreams and hopes. The excuses you accept can begin to seem more real than your purpose. When I first saw kudzu, I thought it was beautiful and impressive. I did not realize that it was deceptive and dangerous. It camouflaged its true nature. The same is true of excuses. An excuse is a reason you give yourself why your dream is no longer valid or possible. It is a mental trick that helps you "give up." It is a way to relieve yourself of responsibility for your mission. It is the "kudzu" of the mind.

The primary problem with excuses is that they create "possibility blindness." The moment you allow excuses to take root, your dream begins to rot. All the wonderful and exciting possibilities you imagined fade into the shadows. Your motivation evaporates, and your energy drops. Excuse momentum carries you back to the bog. It puts your life into reverse. Your choice is simple; you must eliminate your excuses, put your life back into a forward gear, and go for your best dreams.

It is hard to fulfill your purpose. It requires work, sacrifice, and deep commitment. It takes time. It demands your best. Excuses give you "a way out." But if you listen to your excuses and surrender your dream, your soul will shrink. Your life will become empty; you will be disappointed. The "kudzu" is deceptive. It may look beautiful at first, but it covers up the reality of failure. The only way to live a life of purpose, happiness, vitality, usefulness, and meaning is to cut out the "kudzu" of excuses and restart your purpose. Excuses, like kudzu, have a powerful momentum. Once they start, it is hard to stop. Do not let the "kudzu" of excuses steal your dream. Your mission is too important.

CHAPTER 9
How to Lock onto Your Purpose

The Attack of the Death Star

One afternoon, Amy and I were driving through Alabama on our way home to Atlanta. It was a beautiful afternoon in May, and I was listening to a talk show on the radio. The program dealt with entertainment and featured a new movie that was receiving a surge of response from the public. Two film critics gave their views that the movie was so bad they could not understand or explain its popularity. The film was entitled, *Star Wars*. I decided to see the movie as soon as possible.

By the time Amy and I were able to get tickets, it was August. Every showing was sold out for three months. The movie had become a national sensation. Even with tickets, we stood in line for two hours to just enter the theater. When we walked into the auditorium, the only seats left were in a crowded row at the back. I knew nothing about the film apart from the name but was instantly captivated when the now-famous scroll swept upward on the screen. By the time Luke was standing outside his simple home on the planet Tatooine and gazing up at the setting of the double suns, I was hooked.

The action, the never-before-seen special effects, the vivid characters, and the epic story gripped my imagination. I had never seen a film like it (as had no one else). I sat, entranced, as the rebel alliance launched its attack on the death star. It was "David vs. Goliath" in a "galaxy far, far away."

I still recall one dramatic moment when a brave rebel pilot, started his attack run. Fighters from the evil Empire desperately pursued the lone

X-Wing fighter as laser cannon fired bolts of death at the small craft. Just when it seemed that the pilot might abort his attack, the voice of his squadron commander crackled across his communicator. The voice said emphatically, "Stay on target!"

The purpose of this chapter is to help you "stay on target." Once you recognize the signals God is sending you, have found and clarified your purpose, and escaped the detours and roadblocks in your way, you are ready to fulfill that purpose. Life is meaningless unless you fulfill the purpose for which you were born. You must "stay on target." You need a "purpose-lock."

A Positive Program to Pursue Your Purpose

I am going to give you a personal program that can keep you "on target". It gives you specific steps to follow. It is simple and easy to remember.

The Real Estate Lesson

A wise friend told me that when he was 36 years old, the business he had built was profitable enough that he wanted to invest excess funds. He decided to buy real estate but was inexperienced. He made the mistake of broadcasting to his local community his interest in property, and because people knew of his success, he suddenly found that the prices for the properties he wanted to buy were greatly inflated. He learned the lesson that lack of preparation combined with the lack of a plan can lead to disaster.

He decided not to purchase any property until he knew more about the real estate industry. He suspended all his deals and spent the rest of the year studying the real estate market in his area. He scheduled appointments with real estate agents he trusted and "picked their brains." He met with owners of construction companies so he could understand their views on different properties. He created an informal education course for himself and mastered the details of real estate investment. The result was astonishing. He became an "expert" in property evaluation over several months.

When he reentered the market, he was ready for success. He eventually became one of the largest real estate owners in the region. He built hundreds of apartments on land that had been overlooked by other developers. He located these properties that others had missed because he developed an exceptional skill in finding real estate that other people had not noticed. He made multiple millions of dollars.

He was humble enough to recognize his limitations and open enough to learn from other people. Because he had already built a successful international business, he could have assumed that he could automatically succeed at everything else he tried, but he was smart enough to seek help.

His earlier success was based on his work ethic, but his real estate success was founded on his work ethic plus his willingness to prepare and plan.

I urge you to do the same thing. Make the investment to prepare for your life mission and create a plan you can follow. This is what I mean when I say I am giving you "a positive plan to pursue your purpose." A good plan will not only guide you; it will protect you and help you "stay on target."

Here is the plan:

1. Spark Analysis

The Still, Small Voice

Several years ago, I was struggling with a significant decision. I did everything I had learned to do. I researched the options, sought counsel from people I trusted, consulted Amy, and prayed for guidance but could not come to a decision.

I was approaching a deadline and running out of time. I had three days before I had to choose what to do.

Early one morning, I rose at 5:30 to walk and pray. It was a cool misty morning in May as I moved through the silent streets of our small town. I had walked for almost an hour when I became aware of a "still, small voice." I sensed a faint hint of an answer to my urgent questions. As I focused on this inner voice, I was startled to realize that this inner thought had been with me for weeks, but I had dismissed it. I stopped under a streetlight and let the thought grow in my mind. The more I considered this idea, the more I knew that this was my answer and that it had been there the entire time, but I had not listened to it.

Suddenly I knew what to do. I made the decision, and it turned out to be precisely the right choice. The "still, small voice" I experienced was only a spark, but when I analyzed the spark, it grew into a light that revealed what to do.

When you are honest in your heart and have asked God for guidance, then you must be alert for any quiet thoughts or ideas that refuse to go away. Your direction may only be a "spark" in the beginning, but that spark may lead you to the answer you need.

The Exciting Lunch

When I worked with Dr. Charles Stanley, as his special preaching assistant at the First Baptist Church in Atlanta, we sometimes had lunch to discuss plans and projects.

On Wednesday afternoon, we met in the church cafeteria. I was uncertain about direction in a situation and asked for Dr. Stanleys counsel. I expected wise advice and was not disappointed. Dr. Stanley asked me if I had any persistent sense of direction that kept surfacing and would not go away. I admitted that I had been sensing an answer for several days but was uncertain of its dependability. He then told me that, in his experience, one of the tests of God's direction was the consistent return of a thought or idea. That return did not guarantee that the thought was right, but it was a sign that the thought might be one of God's signals, if it would not go away. He stated his belief that God often kept sending the same signal until you received and understood the message. He then told me a story of a significant property negotiation he had conducted for the church. The negotiation stalled, and no one would compromise. One afternoon, sitting in the office of the property developer and his lawyers, Dr. Stanley, said that a small thought that had persisted for weeks, returned and he realized that that idea was what was needed to complete the transaction. He presented his idea, and everyone agreed that it was the answer they had been seeking. The deal was done, and everyone was happy. The result was a great blessing to the church and advanced its growth dramatically.

The lunch had suddenly become exciting and productive. I had learned a valuable lesson in discerning and understanding God's direction.

I am not saying that every stray thought or occasional idea is a signal from God. I am saying that when you have sincerely asked for God's direction, He often responds with thoughts and ideas that will not go away. You usually have a sense of peace and "rightness" connected to the thought or idea that grows over time. That spark may be your answer. You must still analyze and investigate the idea and seek wise, Godly counsel. But if the idea continues to be confirmed, then it may be the spark you need.

Because there is so much competition for your attention, these sparks may be hard to see. Because of that, you should develop a personal "spark sensor." You should spend time every day quietly listening. This "commitment to quiet" is a difficult discipline. The fast pace of modern life and the continual streams of stimulation that flow over you make it hard to stop and listen. When you do stop, you often feel strange and unnatural. When you try to have "quiet time," you can quickly become frustrated and impatient. But this discipline will provide rich rewards and greatly expand and deepen your life.

A Return to Dr. Jones

I am sure you remember the story I told you earlier about my time with Dr. E. Stanley Jones. You may recall that Dr. Jones was a remarkable Christian leader who had developed a program that captivated the intellectual leadership of India. He was a consultant used by both the President of India and the President of the United States. He was friends with Gandhi and the Nehru family, who politically dominated India. Everyone who knew him, loved, and appreciated him.

You may also recall that he told me that early in his ministry, his schedule had become so demanding that his days passed in a blur of action. He failed to recognize the danger of overactivity and slipped into a pattern of shallow thinking. He spent most of his time traveling, speaking, and reacting to events and situations.

He said that he solved this problem by establishing his "listening post" You may remember that he rearranged his daily schedule so he could start the day alone with God for an unhurried time of prayer and reflection.

But something I did not mention is that he told me that his "listening post" was not easy to create or easy to maintain. He said that, at first, it was difficult to stop his thoughts from scattering and his attention from fading, but he persisted.

Because he did not quit, this eventually became the most important and vital part of his day. He began to see solutions to problems that had puzzled him and started to understand principles that he had never thought of before. Decisions became easier. His thinking became increasingly clear. He experienced a deeper calm and peace, and his awareness of God became more real. He said that all the great ideas and successful plans that had altered the direction of his life came from his "listening post." He told me that he still went to his "post" every day and that it was the most valuable hour that he spent.

I have returned to this story because I believe that one of the urgent needs of our time is for leaders to stop and listen. I warn you that it is not easy to turn off the continual stimulation around you and tune into the quiet messages you need. You will struggle with frustration and impatience, but the rewards are enormous. When you learn the "skill of waiting," it will empower your life.

The One Mile Walk

I understood his message because I had learned the same lesson when I was sixteen years old. I had entered a wonderful relationship with Jesus Christ when I was thirteen. I only began to grow in that relationship when I was fifteen and started to study the Bible.

When I turned sixteen, I developed a desire to know God better and decided to learn how to pray. I asked a local pastor if I could use his church after school to pray. He agreed and gave me a key. Every day after school, I walked a mile from the high school to the church.

When I arrived, I unlocked the door, entered the sanctuary, and sat on a front seat. The first day I planned an hour to pray and listen to God. I prayed about everything I could think of, then sat quietly and waited. I estimated that at least thirty minutes had passed, but when I looked at a clock on the wall, only five minutes had expired. I was shocked and frustrated. But I wanted this spiritual experiment to succeed, so I stayed the entire hour.

The next day I hoped the time would go faster but had the same result. I determined to continue. I went to the church every week with a firm commitment to hear from God, but nothing happened. I was a typical high school kid, with high energy and multiple interests. I played basketball and volleyball (I had a great serve) and pursued my growing interest in girls. It was the biggest challenge in my life to that point, to sit quietly for an hour every day. But my desire to know God persisted. I continued to walk the mile to the church every day.

I kept to this schedule for three months until one Monday afternoon, everything changed. I walked to the church, unlocked the door, and went to my usual place. I sat on the front seat, said a prayer, and waited. Suddenly everything was different. God's presence blazed into life. My mind filled with insights and ideas that amazed me. The world began to make sense in ways I had never experienced. My understanding expanded. My emotions soared with joy.

This was the launch of my "listening post". I have been at that post every day now for decades. It is just as powerful now as it was that first moment when my "listening post" came alive.

I am not telling you that you must experience your growth the same as me. But you can still learn the power of quiet. You can develop the discipline of "the pause." You can learn to listen. This is how you can learn to recognize the spark that is trying to get your attention. This is how you can learn to correctly analyze that spark and follow where it leads.

Whatever your beliefs, you can still benefit from the application of these principles. You can create a "listening post" where you can make plans in the calm center of careful and intelligent reflection. You can slow down enough to identify your "sparks" of direction.

2. The Universal Principle of Roots and Fruits

The Garden

Carl is our neighbor. He is friendly and helpful. You could not have a better neighbor. Last week I walked by Carl's house at the end of a street overlooking a bend in a sweeping, deep green river. Carl is a "maximizer" (so is Amy), and he has skillfully maximized his yard by the river into a mix of flower and vegetable garden plots. I enjoy passing his house because different flowers bloom at different times, and the scenery is refreshing (his lush, blue hydrangeas are in full form this week).

As I walked by Carl's house, he rose from one of his vegetable areas and waved. Carl is retired from the U.S military and is still fit and healthy. He asked me if I wanted to have some of the broadleaf lettuce he had just picked. I eagerly agreed. My Great Aunt Lack had fed me the same lettuce she harvested on her farm, smothered in bacon grease (she lived to be 96). It was a happy memory. I carried the stalk of lettuce around the corner to our home and deposited it in the kitchen. It was delicious. The root of the lettuce produced the lettuce we enjoyed for dinner. Without a root, lettuce could not exist. Everything in Carl's garden is dependent on its root system for growth, and the root system would not exist without seeds. The seeds produce the roots, and the roots produce the fruits (by fruits, I mean, results, not necessarily a fruit like an apple or a peach). This means that you must plant the right seeds to grow the right purpose.

One of the best-known verses in the bible explains this principle. Galatians 6:7,9 says, "Do *not be deceived: God cannot be mocked. A man reaps what he sows...Let us not become weary in doing good, for at the proper time we will reap a harvest if we do not give up."*

This is the principle of "sowing and reaping." My friend Charles Stanley says that there is no more reliable principle in the world. He often reminded me that "you will reap what you sow, more than you sow, later than you sow." There is no exception.

This means that whatever seeds you sow today will produce a harvest. Be careful to only sow seeds that improve your life and support your mission. If you sow seeds of gossip and selfishness, you will reap a harvest of bad relationships and unhappiness. If you sow seeds of negative complaining and a belief that you are a victim, then you will reap a harvest of disappointment and anger. If you sow seeds of laziness and disorganization, you will reap a harvest of unpaid bills and disappointments.

But, if you sow seeds of compassion and generosity, you will reap a harvest of friends and prosperity. If you sow seeds of hard work and promise-keeping, you will reap a harvest of success and a good reputation. If you sow seeds of sleep, exercise, and a nutritious diet, you will reap a harvest of good health and a, hopefully, long life. And if you sow seeds of commitment to your calling, you will reap a harvest of a life-purpose, happily fulfilled. Everything depends on the seeds you CHOOSE to sow.

3. The Mirror Technique

Here is a simple way to remind yourself daily of your mission and purpose. After you wake, go to a mirror, look at the reflection, and ask yourself if this is the person you want to be. This is an opportunity to focus on the actions and decisions of the previous day and determine if you have been consistent with your best intentions.

The first time I did this, I felt silly and embarrassed. I looked at myself and laughed. The exercise did not seem serious. But I forced myself to stop, look and think and in a few minutes, I became aware of something I had failed to do the day before that I had promised someone, I would take care of. As I watched myself in the mirror, I realized that I wanted to be a person who was dependable and trustworthy.

The few minutes in front of the mirror helped me reconnect with my expectations of myself. I prayed for help, decided to apologize to the person I had failed, and determined to fulfill my commitments during the new day I was just beginning. Tine "mirror technique did all of this.

4. Symbolism Support

It is essential to surround yourself with reminders of your mission. These "symbols of purpose" help create an atmosphere of encouragement and inspiration.

Surrounded by Eagles

My friend and mentor, Dexter Yager, surrounded himself with images of eagles. When I visited him at his 16,000 square foot "cabin" on Lake Wylie in South Carolina, I drove through custom-built iron gates, shaped as eagles in flight, and drove over a giant, circular mosaic of an eagle embedded in the pavement of his driveway. When I entered the house, there were paintings of eagles and statues of eagles in every room. Dexter chose this symbol as a motivation for success. Of the 60 species of eagle, Dexter selected the American Bald Eagle as his symbol of achievement. The Bald Eagle is the top predator among all birds. The Bald Eagle is powerful and can fly at speeds of 40 mph and dive toward its prey at 100 mph. The grip of an adult Bald Eagle is ten times stronger than an adult human male and exerts a pressure of 400 pounds per square inch. Eagles nest in almost inaccessible locations at high altitudes. Eagles fear nothing. Dexter decided that the powerful, independent, fearless, and free Bald Eagle best represented the person he aspired to be. That is why he surrounded himself with eagles.

The symbols you choose are personal to you. You should select images that motivate you and fit your purpose. I have a picture of Ronald Reagan in my study because his dynamic optimism and positive attitude inspire me. I respect his love he had for the principles of American freedom.

In the bathroom down the hall from the study is a carving of Noah's Ark, with the words, "God Always Keeps His Promises." In my library is a plaque with the Bible verse Philippians 4:19, *"And my God will meet all your needs according to His riches in glory in Christ Jesus,"* (NIV) that God used to guide me through a difficult financial challenge. On a table in my library is a small reproduction of a charming English village that reminds me of my love of travel. A bronze statue of the largest elephant ever seen in Africa that I hand-carried home from the Republic of South Africa, sits on my desk and reminds me of strength and vitality. And, of course, there are various, dramatic statues of mighty Bald Eagles.

Your symbols are physical expressions of your dreams and personality. Use them wisely. Your plan also requires that you evaluate your progress so you can manage your mission.

Mission Management

There are four basic steps for the management of your life mission.

1. Monitor The Vise-Grip

Amy and I were in church one Sunday morning listening to Dr. Stanley. In his sermon, he mentioned a woman who had come to him for counseling. She was puzzled by her difficult circumstances and wanted guidance. Dr. Stanley told her to listen to God so she could avoid God's "vise-grip."

Later that week, I asked Dr. Stanley what he meant by God's "vise-grip." He returned to the story of the woman he had mentioned in the message and told me that she had felt a deep calling to serve God in medicine but had resisted that calling and chosen another direction. She admitted to Dr. Stanley that when she had detoured away from Gods calling, her life had become more and more difficult. She had come to Dr. Stanley for counseling to try to understand her situation.

Dr. Stanley told me that he was sensitive to her suffering but wanted her to know that her wrong choices had put her in God's "vise-grip." He told her that God was using her circumstances to "get her attention" and redirect her to her life purpose. God loved her and did not want her to miss that purpose.

A vise-grip is a tool that can be locked into position to hold another object. It is used to clamp something firmly in place. It is designed to increase pressure as it tightens. This is the image Dr. Stanley used to describe the circumstantial process God uses to "squeeze" you until you understand what He is saying. God uses His "vise-grip" because His message and your mission are that important. Not every difficult circumstance is, of course, a message, but when you are drifting away from your purpose, this is one method God uses to guide you back. This means you should regularly monitor yourself and your circumstances. When an obstacle appears, or a challenge distracts you, examine those things to see if God is trying to show you something. Monitor your schedule and your decisions, so you stay "on target." Monitor your actions, so you maintain momentum toward your mission. Stay alert to the signals God sends to direct you.

2. Measure

The Lunch on Top of an Atlanta Skyscraper

I was invited to lunch by a senior vice-president of one of the largest financial brokerage firms in the United States. He sent me directions to a prominent office building in downtown Atlanta, told me where to park and gave me a special code to give to a security guard when I entered. The guard escorted me to an elevator that carried me to the top floor of the building.

When the door opened, I was greeted by a man in a white jacket who took me to a table with a spectacular view of the city. The man who had invited me was already at the table and rose to welcome me. He was active in the church where I served, and we had known one another for three years. There were other tables occupied by guests and those who had invited them, and everyone spoke in quiet tones and moved with calm efficiency. It was a peaceful and dignified atmosphere.

After a lunch of Caesar salad and fresh lobster, we settled into our conversation. I was curious about why my friend had invited me to such an impressive lunch. I did not have the money to invest at his level of financial involvement and wondered why he wanted to speak with me. A few minutes past dessert (delicious chocolate pecan pie), he told me the reason for our meeting. He was at the top of his profession and a compassionate, caring Christian. He appreciated the potential of my position at the church, and he wanted to give me financial insights and guidance that would not only help me but provide helpful information for those I ministered to, as well. I was dazzled by the high-level knowledge he imparted. His insights were remarkable. I understood why he had achieved all he had.

When he finished, he said that there was one more principle he wanted me to grasp. He had saved it for last because he wanted me to appreciate its importance. He said that all financial success and management started with one thing. Without it, you would eventually fail, but with it, you could succeed. By this time, he had my total attention. Everything he had shared had been fascinating, and I could not think what else was so valuable that he had saved it for such particular emphasis.

I waited, and he said that all financial security begins with measurement. Good record-keeping is essential to financial management. He said that if you do not write down (or in some way record) everything, your decisions will be blind. You will make mistakes and blunders because you cannot build wealth on guesses. He then added that estimates are useless because even smart, experienced people consistently overestimate what they have and underestimate what they owe. Accurate measurement is the foundation of all business success.

I was surprised. I had expected an insight of such depth and power that it would blow everything else away. I was disappointed at first, but as I considered his words, I saw the simple truth of his statements. If you do not know what you are working with, how can you manage it? I realized that he was right; accurate information is the key to every good decision. You should not only monitor your mission, so you do not drift away from your purpose, but you should also regularly measure your progress. You should calculate real numbers and uncover actual details that reveal your direction. This information will inform your decisions and protect your purpose. I recommend that you follow my friend's advice and write down (or record electronically) your progress. When you can see on paper or a screen, exactly what you are doing (or not doing), then you are better equipped to keep your mission on track.

3. Mood

The Lonely Farmhouse

On a November Monday morning during my freshman year in college, I was sitting in the college cafeteria when a senior student walked to my table and sat down. He asked me if I was free for the coming weekend, and I said yes. He then said that he was scheduled to speak at a church in Indiana that weekend but had an unexpected conflict. He asked if I could fill in for him. He barely knew me and had never heard me speak, so I asked why he had chosen me. He gave the vague answer that he "just thought I could do it."

I suspected that one reason he asked was that I was one of the few freshmen with a car. I agreed, and he gave me the address of a family home where I would be staying. He said they would host me and take me to the church for the services.

On Saturday afternoon, I left for a rural community in central Indiana, a few hours from our campus in Kentucky. I was eighteen years old and had rarely been out of my home state. I prayed for God to help me as I drove. The more I prayed, the more I sensed God's blessing. I felt "right" about the opportunity and was excited to speak the next morning.

I arrived around 8 pm, and the family welcomed me and gave me a meal. We visited for an hour, and then they took me to the upper floor of their large, rambling farmhouse. We climbed three staircases until we reached a small bedroom in the attic. They explained that only the first two floors had heat, but the attic bedroom had heavy quilts on the bed that should keep me warm. They left me for the night in a room that was barely big enough for one single bed (with three heavy quilts), a table, and a lamp. I placed my bag at the foot of the bed, undressed and burrowed under the quilts.

At 1 a.m. I woke to a fierce wind whipping along the roof. I crawled from beneath the quilts and looked out the single, small window. It was snowing, and the wind was bending the trees in the front yard. It was cold and dark, and I was suddenly overwhelmed with a feeling of lonely sadness. Doubt flooded my mind. I wished I had never accepted the invitation.

For a moment, I forgot the excitement and certainty I had felt on the drive to Indiana. I was sure I had made a mistake. I sat on the bed and prayed for help and guidance.

Just as suddenly as the feelings of despair had swept over me several minutes before, I felt lifted by God's presence in the room. I experienced a positive peace as an assurance of God's care, and blessing filled my awareness. My earlier confidence returned, and my excitement for the upcoming service was renewed.

The meeting the next morning was excellent. The people were receptive and appreciative. I returned to school with a settled sense of satisfaction. It had been a great experience. I also learned a critical lesson in that lonely farmhouse. Emotions cannot always be trusted. Your feelings can mislead you. You must master your moods to complete your mission. Feelings are notoriously changeable and influenced by outer circumstances. The disorientation of my strange surroundings, the cold and isolation of the attic room, the howling storm, and the experience of waking in the middle of the night all caused my emotions to sink into a pit of depression. My feelings failed because of my circumstances. When I was driving earlier, the sun was shining, my focus was on the excitement of a new adventure, and my positive emotions reflected that reality.

Feelings are molded by everything, from diet to the weather. They are not a reliable foundation for your decisions. Imagine your emotions as the bright, red caboose (or cab) at the end of a train. The caboose (the car at the end of the train) was traditionally painted a bright red or yellow and used as a place of entertainment, rest, and refreshment. It was designed to be festive and fun. But the caboose does not pull the train. That job is done by the powerful engine at the front.

Your thoughts and beliefs are the engines that "pulls your train," and the caboose represents your emotions. The engine of your thoughts guides you, not the caboose. The caboose is valuable, but the engine is vital. There will be times when your emotions tell you to give up, moments when your feelings fail to support your purpose. Those are the times when you should mistrust your emotions and remember the power of your purpose. You should remind yourself of your mission and reconfirm your commitment. Your purpose should control your emotions. Your emotions should never control your purpose. When you refocus on your purpose, your emotions will rearrange themselves to support your purpose.

Ankle Therapy

On Labor Day (a United States holiday every September), I was carrying my daughter Allison's luggage to her car, following a visit, when I stepped on a rock and sprained my ankle. I dropped the bags and fell to the pavement in intense pain. The agony was so bad I thought I would pass out.

Later that week, I went to a clinic operated by my best friend, Dr. Mark Barrett. He examined my swollen and discolored ankle and took an X-Ray. After he read the X-Ray and determined that my ankle was not broken, he arranged for me to meet with a physical therapist who worked at the clinic.

The therapist checked my ankle then gave me some important advice. She told me to follow an exercise routine to move my ankle in different directions several times a day. She said that if I did not follow the program, my ankle would become stiff and immobile, and the longer it was in one position, the harder it would be for my ankle to return to normal. It was crucial that I move my ankle.

The same is true of the pursuit of your purpose. Your mission requires movement. When you stop, you become stagnant. If you stay in one place too long, you can become stuck.

The Vision

The Book of Acts in the Christian New Testament of the Bible was written by the first-century physician Luke (who also wrote the Gospel of Luke). It is a history of the development of the early church.

In Acts 16:6-10, the apostle Paul, the most dominant and important of the early church leaders, had an experience that redirected the expansion of the new Christian movement into Europe. The verses say, *"Paul and his companions traveled throughout the region of Phrygia and Galatia, having been kept by the Holy Spirit from preaching the Word in Asia. When they came to the border of Mysia, they tried to enter Bithynia, but the Spirit of Jesus would not allow them to. So they passed by Mysia and went down to Troas. During the night, Paul had a vision of a man of Macedonia standing and begging, 'Come over to Macedonia and help us'." After Paul had seen the vision, we got ready at once to leave for Macedonia, concluding that God had called us to preach the Gospel to them".*

Not only is this a remarkable description of how God guides those who are listening to Him, but it is also a vivid picture of a commitment to action. It says that "After Paul had seen the vision, WE GOT READY AT ONCE TO LEAVE..." Paul, Luke, and their companions were action oriented. They continually moved toward their mission.

The same is right for you. When you have seen your vision, you should always "move toward your mission." This does not mean that you should never stop and rest. There are strategic moments when you need to pause and renew yourself and your dream. But when that renewal is complete, you need to continue to move forward. Your actions should be DEFINITE, DELIBERATE, AND DECISIVE. After all, you are PURSUING a purpose.

The most essential fact about your purpose is that it is important. Whatever you are meant to do matters, not only for your personal happiness but for the welfare and benefit of other people. If you want to live a life of satisfaction and purpose, then do these three things:

- Discover your purpose,

- Follow your purpose, and

- Fulfill your purpose. Nothing matters more.

The Fire

On May 20, 2020, while working on this book, our home caught on fire. Our son, Jonathan, was participating in an on-line Law School class, smelled smoke, and called the fire department. Our lives were saved by minutes.

The damage to our 100-year-old home was extensive. Although the fire department saved the structure, our entire second floor was almost destroyed. All our clothing was lost, along with valuable paintings and memorabilia we had collected around the world. Numerous family pictures melted.

The shock and trauma ripped into our lives, but three things remained constant our family and friends, God's love and provision, and OUR PURPOSE. During this challenging experience, our family and friends have become more precious, our relationship with God has become more profound and more powerful, and our purpose has become more apparent and more compelling. We have learned that God's promises are ALWAYS true and that God's purpose for you never changes. We are happier than ever.

Keep believing, no matter what happens, your purpose still matters. It is the reason you are alive. Our unexpected circumstances have only clarified and re-ignited our purpose. We are more committed to that purpose than ever.

This book exists because of my conviction that God has called me to help you find and fulfill YOUR purpose. The meaning of your life is your mission. Whatever that mission is, it matters. It is what you are SUPPOSED to do. People need you to accomplish it.

- Make a commitment today to be true to your purpose.

- Learn to recognize the signals that are being sent to you.

- Dedicate yourself to becoming the person you need to be to complete your purpose.

- Overcome every obstacle in your way.

- Monitor your progress and follow your plan.

- Discover your purpose and bless the world.